LEARN UPHOLSTERY

Desmond Gaston

COLLINS

Contents

The author and publishers would like to thank the following people for lending furniture and for help in many other ways. Maureen Braham, Caroline Harris, Ted Collins, Maureen and Malcolm Smith, Jill Martin, Mr and Mrs Patrick Smith and Miss N. Roberts.

First published in 1989
by William Collins Sons & Co Ltd
London · Glasgow · Sydney · Auckland · Johannesburg

Series Editor Eve Harlow
Designed by Mike Leaman
Text editor Flicka Lister
Illustrated by Tig Sutton, Stan North
Colour artwork by Antonia Enthoven
Photographs: Richard Palmer pages 5, 7, 35, 61;
Bert Braham pages 12, 20, 27, 31, 33, 45, 51, 57;
Downing Street Studios, Farnham, page 43; Elizabeth
Whiting Associates pages 47, 48–49; Sanderson's
Fabrics pages 9, 41, 63.
Cover photograph by Alan Duns

Note: Some of the material in this book has previo
been published in 'Upholstery – A Practical Guide'
Desmond Gaston

British Library Cataloguing in Publication Data
Gaston, Desmond
 Learn upholstery.
 1. Upholstering –. Amateurs' Manuals
 I. Title
 645'. 4

ISBN 0–00–412334–4

Typeset by Nene Phototypesetters Ltd, Northamp
Printed by New Interlitho, Italy

Introduction

ou read through this book and follow the
ects and detailed instructions contained in it,
't be surprised if, like so many others who
e set out to learn this traditional and rewarding
t, you soon become a compulsive
olsterer. There is something about upholstery
attracts and, particularly for practically-
ded people, it quickly becomes a compelling
by. It is a craft in which you 'sculpt' with
erials and into which you can put a great deal
our own personality. Like me, I hope you will
joy and satisfaction in tacking, tying, shaping,
ing and fitting to create something that brings
ose.
may be that the materials we use in
olstery – webbing, hessians, springs, and
rent kinds of fillings, will be items of mystery
ou when you first take a piece of furniture
rt. However, you will soon find that seeing
e things go together to form beautifully soft,
ngy furniture is fascinating and thrilling work.
this book there are nine projects and if you

undertake them in order, they will introduce you
gradually to the basic skills you need to learn.
Your own pieces of furniture are unlikely to look
exactly like those pictured but you should be able
to adapt the procedures to suit them.

Before starting a project, glance through the
pages, looking at the diagrams and reading the
captions. Take particular note of the Basic Skills
sections. Each of the projects lists the particular
skills involved and also tells you the tools you
require and which materials you need to buy.

If you can find a chair with a pincushion seat,
such as that pictured on page 22, this would
make a good starting project. Failing this, a chair
with a drop-in seat, such as that on page 27,
would enable you to practise a number of the
basic techniques.

I hope that this book will contribute towards the
teaching of correct, traditional upholstery skills.
I hope it will also bring you the great satisfaction
and enjoyment that comes from producing a first
class piece of upholstery.

Tools, Equipment and Materials

The hand tools required for upholstery are fairly simple ones and are not very expensive to buy. In this section, the basic tools and equipment you need are listed and their uses are described, together with advice about choosing a suitable place to work. Upholstery fabrics are also discussed and there is a useful glossary of trims.

Basic tools

The first task when starting any reupholstery project is the unpicking and ripping off of old materials, so the tools for this job are very important.

Tools for destruction

Knives
A collection of sharp knives is essential for slashing away old coverings, hessians and twines.

Ripping chisel
This is used for getting out old tacks easily and quickly and you will need two, one with a wide blade, the other with a narrow one. The ripping chisel is used with a small mallet.

Pair of pincers
A small pair of pincers is also useful for removing tacks. Choose a pair with the jaws ground on the underside with no bevel on the top faces so that they will remove tacks, nails and pins that are close to the wood.

Side-cutting pliers
A pair of pliers, adapted by grinding the jaws to a point when closed, is very useful for removing awkward tacks. The points can be dug into the wood around a tack head and the tack is then extracted with ease.

Tack-lifter
This should have a well-defined crook and is essential for extracting decorative dome-headed chair nails.

Tools for construction

Scissors
Two different types of scissors are needed.

Cutting out shears Use these for making long, straight cuts in covering fabrics, hessians, linings etc.

Small, pointed trimmers These are used for making small cuts, trimming surplus fabric, and for fitting upholstery fabric. They are also useful for unpicking.

Hammers
Several different types of hammer are used in upholstery.

Upholsterer's hammer This has a head and claw and is used for general purposes.

Magnetic hammer This will hold a tack on its face and is useful for those places where fingers cannot reach. It is also invaluable for picking up dropped tacks.

Cabriole hammer This hammer is used for fine tacking work around and near 'show wood' (polished, surface wood), and for tacking into rebates where a larger-headed hammer might cause damage to the woodwork.

Heavy hammer A slightly heavier, larger-faced hammer is also useful for when tacks need to be driven well home, as when fastening webbing.

Webbing stretchers
There are several types of webbing stretchers (two are illustrated in the picture on page 5, the hinged stirrup type and the steel-jawed stretcher). T hinged stirrup type is generally considered the best. The webbing is looped beneath the stirrup and the hinge action pinches and grips the webbing. The third type is the slot an peg stretcher.

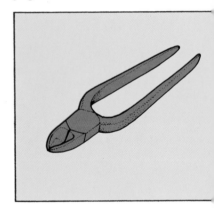

Fig 1 *Side-cutting pliers, adapted by grindir the jaws to more of a point*

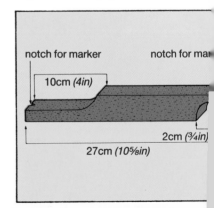

Fig 2 *A special upholstery gauge (designe the author) for gauging guide lines*

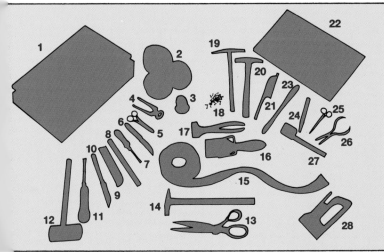

Key to illustration

1 Toolbox; **2** Twines; **3** Sewing thread;
4 Pincers; **5** Small trimming scissors;
6 Sharp cutting knife; **7** Tack lifter;
8 Tack lifter; **9 and 10** Knife and scabbard;
11 Ripping chisel; **12** Mallet;
13 Cutting out shears; **14** Large hammer;
15 Webbing; **16** Webbing stretcher (hinged stirrup type);
17 Steel-jawed webbing stretcher (hide strainers);
18 Tacks; **19** Cabriole hammer;
20 Magnetic claw hammer; **21** Upholstery gauge;
22 Upholstery needles; **23** Button fold stick;
24 Felt-tipped marker; **25** Trimming scissors;
26 Duck-billed pliers (for stretching fabric);
27 Flexible steel tape rule; **28** Staple gun

Needles

The different needles required for upholstery can be seen in the top right of the picture on page 5.

Mattress needles You will need three sizes of these double-pointed needles: a very long one, 35cm *(14in)* in length and of 12 gauge thickness; one of medium length, 25cm *(10in)* long and 13 gauge thickness; and a short one, 20cm *(8in)* and 14 gauge thickness.

Spring needle This curved spring needle has a bayonet point and is used for sewing or fastening webbing or hessian to springs. Choose one that measures 12.5 *(5in)* or 15cm *(6in)* in length.

Semi-circular needles Larger ones 13 or 15cm *(5 or 6in)* are used for sewing with twine. The size is determined by the length of the needle measured round the curve. If possible, also buy one with a point at each end for edge-stitching on chair frames that have show wood surrounding the upholstery. For sewing with thread, much smaller curved needles are required.

Bayonet point curved needle You will need one 7.5cm *(3in)* long, 17 gauge thickness, for use on tough materials such as leather.

Round point curved needles For general upholstery work, choose one 6cm *(2½in)* long, 17 gauge, and another 7.5cm *(3in)* long, 17 gauge.

Curved cording needles These fine needles are used for sewing on decorative chair cord and for sewing on braid and fringe. They tend to break easily but they are not expensive and it is worth buying two or three of 7.5cm *(3in)* length, 19 gauge.

Regulators

These instruments have a number of uses – for packing and distributing stuffing, for marking, and they are also used in buttonwork. The regulator is also very useful as an 'extra finger' for holding covering fabric while fixing it.

Pins and skewers

Upholsterer's pins are long – at least 4cm *(1½in)*. Skewers are 7.5cm *(3in)* or 10cm *(4in)* long. Both are used for

Underside of stool showing basic support of webbing and heavy hessian

temporarily holding and fixing coverings, hessians, etc, and in cushion work.

Measuring and gauging

Rules, measures and straight edges are all used in upholstery work.

Steel tape rule Nearly all measurements in upholstery involve distances round and over curved surfaces so the measuring tape must be flexible.

Yardstick As well as a yardstick's obvious purpose for measuring lengths of cloth, webbing, hessian, etc., it is also very useful as a straight edge.

Upholstery gauge

This is a useful upholstery tool, that you can make yourself (see page 4, Fig. 2).

It was designed as a gauge for drawing guide lines on the first stuffing upholstery scrim for lines of stitches and ties. Cut it from 2cm *(¾in)*-thick wood with a small coping saw, fret saw or hand saw. The notches at each end are made with a rat-tail file or cut as Vs with a small saw. The diagram shows the dimensions for this particular gauge, which will serve most purposes.

Staple gun

A staple gun is shown in the picture on page 5. This is used a great deal in modern upholstery and can be a great time saver, although it has not actually been used for any of the projects in this book. If you decide to buy one, take a piece of hardwood with you to the shop and try out the stapler. Some have very light springs which are of no use except on softwood. Fire a staple into your piece of hardwood and, if the gun is a good one, the staple will be driven well home. The gun should take thin 6mm *(¼in)* staples.

Button-fold sticks

You need two of these and you can make them yourself from pieces of smooth hardwood. For each stick, cut piece of wood about 20cm *(8in)* long, 4mm *(³/₁₆in)* in thickness and 13mm *(½in)* in width. Shape with glass pape so that one end is a smooth point. Round off the corners at the other end You will also need a few sundry items such as felt-tipped pens and markers.

A place to work

The initial stages of stripping down a piece of furniture is dirty work. There will be a lot of dust and debris. An outhouse or garage converted into a workshop is best but if this is not possible, do the stripping down job outdoors, then bring your piece of furniture indoors for upholstery.

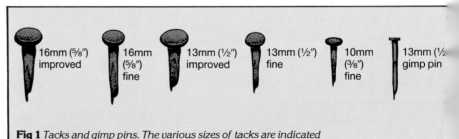

16mm *(⅝")* improved   16mm *(⅝")* fine   13mm *(½")* improved   13mm *(½")* fine   10mm *(⅜")* fine   13mm *(½ gimp pin*

Fig 1 *Tacks and gimp pins. The various sizes of tacks are indicated*

Basic equipment

Trestles

It is important for both comfort and efficiency to have your work at the right height and professional upholsterers use trestles of different heights: a pair of high trestles for working on seats of easy chairs; a medium-height pair for working on arms, and a pair of low trestles for working on backs and wings. Trestles usually have a groove or trough in the top surface to take the castors or legs, thus preventing the furniture from moving during working.

A 'Workmate'

The piece of equipment called commercially a 'Workmate' (see the picture on this page), is a very useful accessory for the home upholsterer. A table top can be clamped to the top and this is useful for working on single chair seats or stools, as the legs can be adjusted to two heights. The lower position is used when ripping off, fixing webbing or putting on stuffing, while the higher level makes edge-stitching, covering and trimming easier.

Work tables

Old kitchen tables can sometimes be purchased quite cheaply and these can easily be converted for use as work surfaces. They should be not less than 5cm (30in) square. Screw 3cm (1/4in) – square wooden battens all round the top edges – these will prevent the furniture from slipping off during working.

You will need two converted tables, one high enough for you to be able to work on chair seats and another with the legs cut down so that it stands over, for working chair backs and arms.

Old plywood-topped folding card tables can also be adapted for work tables.

Cutting out tables

You can use the floor for cutting out from lengths of fabric but if you are going to do a lot of upholstery you may find this both inconvenient and uncomfortable. A serviceable cutting-table can be made by setting a 2.4 × 1.2m (8 × 4ft) sheet of 13mm

A 'Workmate' is a useful piece of equipment in upholstery. Clamp a table top to the top surface for working single chairs.

(1/2in)-thick plywood onto a framework of 2.5 × 5cm (1 × 2in) soft wood battens, and resting this across the top of the high trestles. This will prove extremely useful for cutting out covering fabrics and for other table top jobs.

You will also need the use of a domestic sewing machine.

Materials and sundries

Webbing

Webbing is a basic support in a piece of upholstered furniture and needs to be strong enough to bear the weight of the person using the chair or sofa. The best and longest-lasting webbing is 5cm (2in) black and white, woven from strong cotton, sometimes with man-made fibres mixed in for extra strength.

Rubber webbing Many modern upholstered chairs have rubber webbing for their seat platforms, usually of 5cm (2in) width. Rubber webbing makes a comfortable and efficient base for a cushioned seat but will need replacing after three to four years of use. Metal clips are supplied for fastening the ends of the webbing straps and this makes for easy fixing.

Heavy tarpaulin hessian

This fabric is used as a platform over the webbing or to cover upholstery springs. The 450g (16oz) weight tarpaulin is recommended.

Lightweight hessians and undercovering fabrics

For the first stuffing covering, a strong scrim hessian is needed. This is a very pliable canvas for forming edge shapes.

For bottom coverings and for reinforcing outside arm and back panels, a 280g (10oz) hessian is used. An inexpensive but strong black cotton lining is sometimes preferred for bottom covering.

For upholstery undercovering you will need a good quality unbleached calico.

Springs

There are three main forms of springs, but only one has been used in this book.

Upholstery coil spring This is the most common form and is also one of the earliest types of spring.

Cords, twines and threads

Laid cord This is a thick cord, usually made of hemp or jute and is used for lacing springs together.

Twine This comes in several thicknesses: **No. 1** (the stoutest) is used for tying springs to webbing and hessian, and for fastening tufts and buttons. **No. 2**, **No. 3** and **No. 4** are finer twines and are used for edge-stitching and for sewing hessians.

It is a good idea to keep a lump of beeswax with your twines and use it to dress them. This will preserve and strengthen them. To dress twine, draw the beeswax along the length of the cut piece, using some pressure.

Nylon tufting twine This is the best cord to use for buttonwork. It tends to be expensive but it is very strong.

Threads

For most jobs in upholstery, cotton thread **No. 18** (very strong), **No. 25** (thinner) and **No. 24** (general purpose) will be sufficient.

Tacks

There are two varieties of upholstery tack (see page 6, Fig 1). The stouter tacks with larger heads are termed 'improved' and those with smaller heads are called 'fine'.

When buying tacks, refer to them as 'cut tacks'.

16mm (⅝in) improved tacks These are the largest tacks and are used mostly for fastening webbing.

16mm (⅝in) fine tacks These tacks can be used for fastening webbing or heavy support hessian when the wood of the frame is liable to split if stouter tacks are used.

13mm (½in) improved tacks These are used for general tacking through thick covering fabric or multi-thicknesses of fabric.

10mm (⅜in) fine tacks These are the smallest tacks used in upholstery, although 6mm (¼in) tacks can be obtained for very delicate work.

Gimp pins These are very fine tacks and are not only used for fixing gimp or braid, but are also useful for general tacking purposes on delicate woodwork. They come in japanned black, white and various colours.

Adhesives

Impact adhesive is used for attaching braids and trimmings. The impact fastness of this glue is retarded so that trimmings can be adjusted before they became firmly fixed. The adhesive is thixotropic (jelly-like) for easy application.

Fillings

Horsehair and sheep's wool These are the best stuffings so if you find them in an old chair, do clean and re-use them for your new upholstery. They can be handwashed in small quantities but a quicker method is to place the hair (or wool) in an old pillowcase, secure the end firmly so that none of the filling escapes, and then put it in the washing machine.

Vegetable fibres These are also worth saving and re-cycling. They are very durable stuffings and can be re-carded successfully. Cotton and wool and cotton felt stuffings can also be re-carded and used as top stuffings.

Upholstery foam

You are advised to avoid all polyurethane (polyether) foams. The use of all but the flame-retardent type i illegal in some countries. Choose instead latex rubber block foam. It will last far longer than plastic foam and is pleasant to use. Latex rubber block foam comes in 2.5cm (1in), 5cm (2in 7.5cm (3in) and 10cm (4in) thicknesse

Waddings, felt, acrylic wool These are used on top of the stuffing to achieve a smooth, soft surface. It is a good idea buy the best quality which should be evenly-textured with no lumps or foreign bodies in it. Wadding comes in rolls and the best quality can be split c opened up still further, to make a widt of about 90cm (36in).

Fabrics and trimmings

Fabrics suitable for covering upholstered furniture are many and varied and, like everything else, the be quality is usually the most expensive. Fabrics containing some wool fibres are the most durable and keep their good looks longest but many fabrics made of man-made fibres are also strong, soft and wear well.

Silk velvet There is nothing as luxurious as real silk velvet, but it is very expensive.

Jacquards Jacquard is the name given to a type of fabric in which the design is incorporated into the weave instead of being printed or dyed onto the surface. The term tends to be used for any patterned fabric that cannot be otherwise classified.

Choosing fabrics

When choosing an upholstery fabric, the first things you will consider are the colour and texture. You should also give some thought to its suitability for your life style and the amount of wear the chair or sofa is likely to get.

Fabrics containing a high proportion of wool, cotton or viscose will feel and look pleasant and are strong and hard-wearing.

Nylon fabrics often look good and are undoubtedly hard-wearing but they tend to attract static electricity, causing particles of grime to adhere to the surface.

Always study the information given on the label when considering a fabric.

Printed fabrics
Some manufacturers cover upholstered furniture with thin, cotton-printed fabrics but this type of fabric is not recommended. This does not mean that you cannot choose a printed fabric. Look for good-quality, thick, printed linens or linen mixtures which will last and always look good.

Trimmings

Beautiful trimmings, carefully chosen to enhance your upholstery work, will give an elegant finishing touch to every project you undertake. A selection of popular braids, cords, fringes and decorative finishes is illustrated on page 10.

Covered buttons
Button making presses are very expensive items so you will find it more convenient to have covered buttons made for you. Shops and store departments specialising in upholstery often provide customers with a button-making service.

Some designs in specialist fabric ranges come in both upholstery qualities and in lighter weights, the latter being more suitable for making matching curtains and cushions.

Tapestry The best is made of wool or a cotton and wool mixture and a good quality tapestry is a durable, thick, closely woven fabric. Tapestry is made in both traditional and modern designs.

Quilted tapestry This is tapestry woven in two layers, which are interwoven in places, giving the fabric an embossed look.

Brocatelle This is a type of brocade fabric with a design woven in relief using both glossy and dull yarns.

Damask Many damasks are plain, one-coloured fabrics with the design created by changes in the weave, but striped damasks are also available.

Cotton velour This is a type of velvet with a close pile. It has a rich, luxurious look but tends to 'shade' with use, especially on chair seats.

Dralon velvet This popular fabric comes in many textures and finishes such as ribbed pile, corduroy, slub pile and even a dull, suede leather look. Dralon is durable and very easy to clean.

Mohair velvet This fabric has a shaggy look but is beautifully soft to the touch.

Trimmings

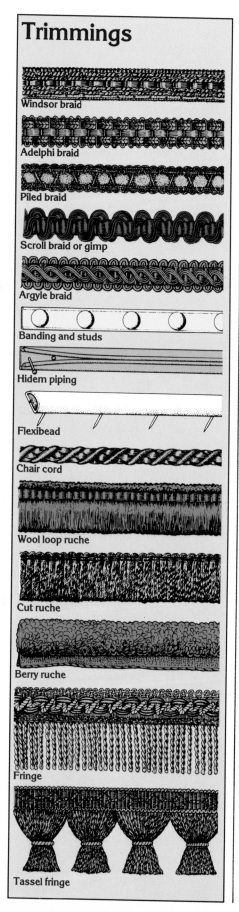

Windsor braid

Adelphi braid

Piled braid

Scroll braid or gimp

Argyle braid

Banding and studs

Hidem piping

Flexibead

Chair cord

Wool loop ruche

Cut ruche

Berry ruche

Fringe

Tassel fringe

Basic Skills 1

Whether the piece you are re-upholstering is a simple stool or something more complicated, like an armchair, measure up for the new fabric while the furniture still has some shape. Use a flexible steel rule which can be bent to follow the curves of the upholstery.

Measuring up for fabric

Before you begin, draw a chart similar to Fig 1. Jot the measurements on this as you take them.

You will not, of course, require all these measurements for, say, an armless chair but the purpose of this section is to show you the basics of measuring up. Next, having chosen the fabric, note the way the pattern runs. With some flowery designs it can be difficult to decide which is the right way up, but if you remember that the buds go at the top and the stalks go at the bottom, you should have little difficulty. With pile fabrics, such as velvet, the pile or nap should always run downwards. On the arms and inside back, it should run down towards the seat, while on the seat it should run from back to front.

Most furnishing fabrics come in 132–137cm *(52–54in)* widths. The new upholstery will in all probability be fuller than the old, so allow for this when taking measurements by holding the tape just above the surface.

Begin by measuring the inside back of the chair and also measure the width to determine whether a half-width of fabric will reach across. On the chair in the illustration it will, which means that the inside and outside back coverings will come from one complete width of fabric.

On the chair illustrated (Fig 2), the inside arms also take only half a width

of fabric each but on a larger chair a full width might have to be allowed for each arm.

Do not consider joining pieces of fabric to make arm coverings – it never looks good.

When taking the arm measurements, tuck the tape well down into the seat side crevice so that it touches the tacking bar. Allow 2.5cm *(1in)* beyond this. Under the top roll-over of the back and arms, allow 2.5cm *(1in)* more than where the outside panel joins. For the outside arms, allow 5cm *(2in)* more than the exact measurement. Refer to the illustration Fig 2.

Next, measure the seat from back to front, tucking the tape well into the back seat crevice and into the front. Allow for the fact that the old seat may have been pushed back considerably through years of use and also that it is probably not the height it should be. There will be almost half a width of fabric left over from the seat – enter this on your chart for 'offcuts'.

The seat border will come from a full width of fabric. Allow enough for turning in at the top and for tacking under the front rail.

At this point, look at the offcuts of fabric you are likely to be left with. You will probably find that you have enough to cover the front arm scroll facings and the two scrolls on each side of the back. Remaining offcuts could be used for piping.

Cushion

Measure for the cushion allowing 2.5cm *(1in)* for the seams. The top and bottom panels will cut from one full width. For the cushion border, measure the four sides, then for each border piece that has to be joined add 2.5cm *(1in)* to the total measurement. Measure the depth of the cushion and add 2.5cm (1in).

Pattern matching

If the design has large repeats, allow at least one repeat extra. If the fabric you are using has a motif that needs to be placed centrally on the back, seat and on the arms, then you should allow extra fabric for this.

With a simple, continuous pattern, allow an extra 50cm *(20in)* on the length. Larger pattern repeats will need an extra allowance – about 75cm *(30in)*.

Cut	Length	Off cuts	
		Length	Width
inside back			
outside back			
inside arms			
outside arms			
seat			
front border			
cushion			
scroll fronts			
piping			
Total			

Fig 1 Chart for noting chair measurements

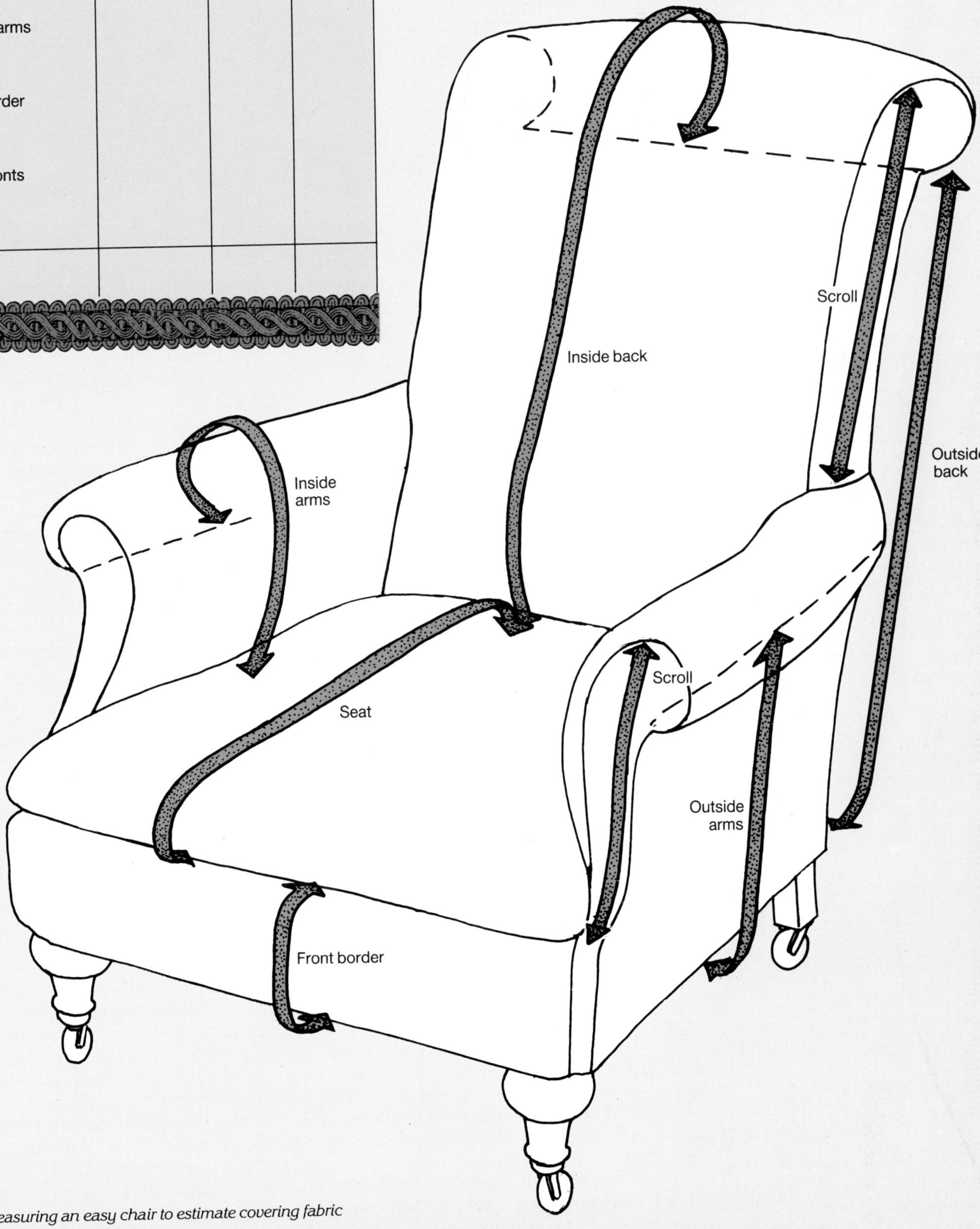

Fig 2 Measuring an easy chair to estimate covering fabric

Choosing Furniture for Upholstery

It is not always easy to tell good quality from bad when looking at old furniture for reupholstering, particularly if most of the wood is covered up. This chapter tells you the signs to look for which will indicate whether a particular piece is a good buy and worthy of an upholstery project, or not.

A great deal can be deduced from the legs. First, the design and turnings are clues as to the age of the chair but, as well as denoting the period, the legs can also indicate the quality – or lack of quality – of the piece.

It helps to be able to identify the various woods because the type used can be a guide to the quality. Better chairs have legs made from hardwoods such as mahogany, walnut, rosewood, oak or the finer birch woods. On cheaper chairs, beech turned legs were often used, the wood stained and polished to look like a better quality wood.

Look at the back legs of chairs. If the wood is the same as that of the front legs it is a good sign. Some back legs are made of beech, which means that the maker used the extension of the back upright for the back legs and did not take the trouble to join on pieces of hardwood. The shape of the back legs is important, too, and it is a good sign if they have a well-defined curve.

Next, examine the castors. A manufacturer proud of his work would always fit chair legs with good-quality brass castors with brass or porcelain bowls, but check that they are the originals. You can do this by inspecting the screws that fasten the castors to the legs to see if they have been disturbed at any time.

It is a good idea to check the size of the wood used for the frame, especially the seat frame. Place your hand under the seat edge and try and judge the dimensions of the wood. It should be at least 4.5–5cm *(1¾–2in)*-square in section, for this is where the strength of the frame needs to be.

At this stage, you may have established that the quality of the chair is good but the joints of the frame may be in poor condition. This can be judged by the amount of movement there is in the arms and back when sideways, back and forward pressure is applied. However, movement in these areas should not depress you too much and put you off the project.

When the chair is completely

Dining chair of Regency period with the seat rails very distressed by age, woodworm and many re-upholsterings

Left: eighteenth-century dining chair

Right: sturdy, well-made mid-nineteenth century single chair

Below: the frame of a 'crinoline' chair of good design and construction

Above: Victorian 'spoon back' chairs of different designs

stripped of its upholstery, the loose frame joints can easily be dismantled and re-glued to give the structure its original firmness.

Chairs with polished show wood

Victorian spoon back chairs come into this category and, usually, there is a great deal of polished wood showing. Test the frame and joints for robustness first. Then look at the sweep of the moulded show wood around the back. Check to see if it is evenly-curved and whether the two sides match. If there is carving, look for delicacy in its execution.

The front legs and front facing wood to the arms should also be elegantly carved or turned.

The size and appearance of the back legs are good indicators of quality. On the best chairs, the back legs have a well-defined curve or ogee (double-curved) shape, and will be about 5cm (2in)-square in section. The legs on poorer quality chairs will look skimpy and weak in comparison.

Dining chairs

In chairs of all ages and periods, the

Holes and filling them

Rails of chairs and other items of furniture can look rather poor when all the old tacks have been taken out. The entire surface may be covered in old tack holes, especially if the piece has been upholstered several times.
However, because tacks are wedge-shaped, although the holes appear large on the surface, the wood deeper down should be more or less intact.

If the holes are so numerous that they cause difficulty when it comes to fastening the new upholstery, make up a filler using PVA glue (white liquid wood glue) and fine band saw sawdust. Mix these together to a fairly wet paste and press this well into the holes with a stiff-bladed palette knife. Allow about 24 hours for the filler to set before commencing the new upholstery.

quality of craftsmanship and design can vary from extremely poor to truly excellent. Many eighteenth-century dining chairs show their lack of quality by the number of times they have had to be repaired, indicating either a poor

choice of wood or an impractical design at outset. On the other hand, servant's hall dining chairs of the late nineteenth century often have all the marks of clever craftsmanship in the symmetry of their shape and the precision in leg turnings and joinery.

Chaises longues and couches

There are many forms and shapes of chaises longues and couches that are of good design and high quality but, equally, there are almost as many pieces where the quality and design are extremely poor.

Pieces with skimpy legs and poor quality castors should be avoided, as should couches with turned spindles in the back that are of unequal shape or size, or those pieces with show wood carving that appears to be simply scratched in, instead of being crisply carved.

Check the thickness of the seat rails (some are so poor that they may be no more than 2.5cm (1in) in thickness). This could mean that, although there appears to be an even depth of border and edge to the seat, it is only because rough wooden battens have been

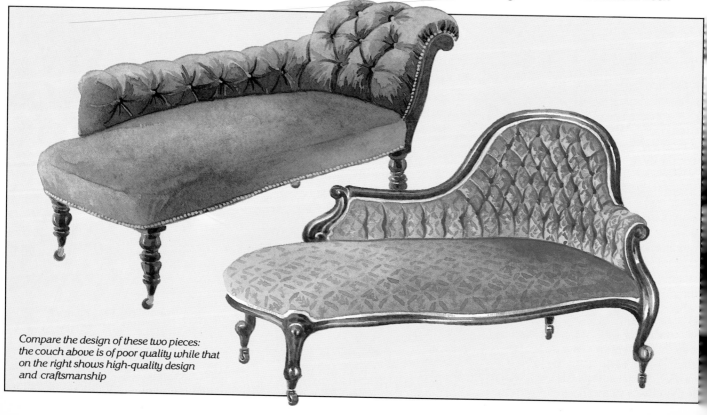

Compare the design of these two pieces: the couch above is of poor quality while that on the right shows high-quality design and craftsmanship

nailed around to give the seat its required depth.

Iron-framed chairs and couches

Good quality iron-framed or part iron-framed furniture will have been made of stout 13mm *(1/2in)* mild steel bar and steel strips of stout, unbendable gauge. Try to discover (by feeling through the old upholstery) whether the frame is of this nature. Also, push and pull the back to see how much movement there is. This will also tell you how well the iron structure has been made. The legs and castors again are a useful indication of the quality of workmanship.

Examining for woodworm

When examining dining chairs, always turn them upside down and look at the underside. It is wise to be suspicious of any loose-seated chairs or stuffed-over chairs that have the bottoms covered over with black lining fabric or hessian, because the last upholsterer may have had something to hide — such as a bad infestation of woodworm. A good craftsman will leave the bottom of the chair open and uncovered so that the quality of his work can be seen.

Black lacquered beechwood chairs or sofas in particular should be examined very carefully for signs of woodworm. Beechwood is particularly vulnerable to woodworm, but the lacquer hides the damage with few holes showing on the surface. You can be totally unaware of the situation until suddenly a leg breaks to reveal a honeycomb of holes within. Always examine both ends of legs and tap the wood with your fingers to see if any sign of hollowness can be heard.

It is also difficult to tell if woodworm is in the frame of a completely stuffed-over easy chair (particularly if the legs are made of mahogany or rosewood, which woodworm does not often attack). Legs made of oak, walnut, birch or beech would probably show signs of infestation — and just one or two holes could mean that the inside of the chair is completely riddled with woodworm. If woodworm is detected in the frame, then the frame test described for the stuffed-over easy chair should be carried out to assess possible damage to the chair's strength.

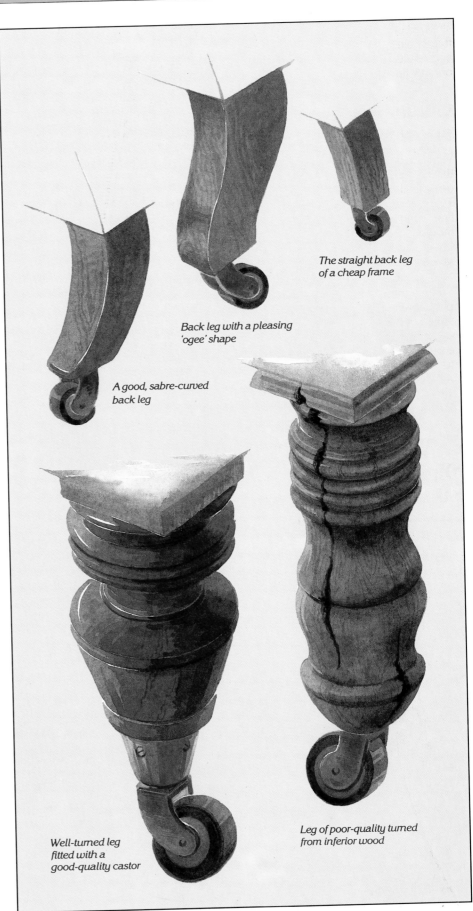

The straight back leg of a cheap frame

Back leg with a pleasing 'ogee' shape

A good, sabre-curved back leg

Well-turned leg fitted with a good-quality castor

Leg of poor-quality turned from inferior wood

Basic Skills 2

Preparing to work

On this page and also on page 18, you are shown how to tackle the necessary preparation work that must be done before starting the actual upholstery. The first stage of the work is called 'ripping off', when the old fabric and filling is removed. Then, after a good brush down, the piece of furniture will be ready for the new webbing. In this section, the various knots used in upholstery are also explained.

Preparation

Before removing the old covering it is always a good idea to study the piece, its shape and construction. You may want to change the style of the upholstery in some way, for example, by putting in a buttoned back. This is the best time to think about the potential of your piece of furniture.

Now, measure the piece, following the instructions on page 10. This will help you to assess the amounts of hessian, undercovering and covering fabrics you will be needing later.

Ripping off

Tools required
Ripping chisel, mallet, sharp knife, scissors, adapted side-cutting pliers.

There will be a considerable amount of dust and dirt in the furniture and it is therefore advisable to wear a cotton mask.

Here is the stripping procedure for a single chair that has no springs. With the chair the right way up, cut away the covering fabric and remove the upholstery layer by layer, using a ripping chisel and mallet, knife and scissors.

For a sprung single chair or a dining room chair, begin with the chair upside down and rip off the bottom covering and webbing. Remove the springs and then, with the chair the right way up, take out the rest of the seat.

The sequence of stripping a fully-upholstered easy chair is as follows: do the underside of the seat first, then the outside back, the outside arms, the remaining seat upholstery, the back upholstery and, lastly, the two arms.

As you remove the old upholstery layer by layer, observe how it was done before. By doing this (and by being critical) you can learn a lot.

If you're lucky, there will be horsehair in good condition that can be recarded. Put this in an old pillowcase or plastic bag to deal with later (refer to Fillings, page 8).

Using the ripping chisel
The ripping chisel, used with a small mallet, considerably speeds up the process of removing the old tacks but care must be taken when using this tool or you may damage the woodwork.

Place the blade of the chisel against the tack head and drive the chisel with the mallet (Fig 1). As the tack begins to lift, lower the chisel handle and continue to drive it, but more gently, to remove the tack (Fig 2). Keep your eye on the tack and not on the chisel, and do not hold your face directly over the work because tacks can suddenly fly up and, sometimes, the heads come off as well. Try to 'rip' in the direction of the grain to avoid too much damage and if fragments of wood do split from the frame, glue them back immediately.

Use the adapted side pliers to clear the tacks from delicate woodwork such as the wood near to the front leg joints.

If there appears to be a large number of holes from previous upholstery, they can be filled using the PVA and sawdust mixture described on page 14.

Knots in upholstery

Various kinds of knots are used by professional upholsterers and are referred to in the projects in this book. It is a good idea to become proficient in tying them before starting your first project.

Reef knot (Fig 3)
This is used for joining cords of equal thickness and the rule is 'left over right and right over left'. The reef knot is not used very often but it is useful if you misjudge the length of cord required and need to join in an extra piece. The knot can also be used to tie off cottons and twines at the end of a row of stitches.

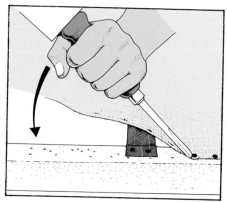

Fig 1 *Place the chisel blade against the tack head and drive it with the wooden mallet*

Fig 2 *As the tack begins to lift, lower the chisel handle and drive the mallet more gently*

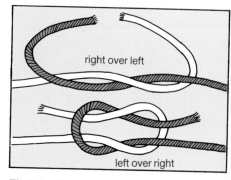

right over left

left over right

Fig 3 Reef knot: *pass the left hand cord over the right hand cord, then the right over the left (3a). Repeat the procedure as shown, then pull the ends to tighten the knot (3b)*

1. Pass the left hand cord over the right hand cord and the right hand cord over the left (Fig 3a).
2. Fig 3b shows the second stage of the knot, where the process is repeated.
3. Pull the ends to tighten the knot.

Sheet bend (Fig 4)
This is used for joining cords of unequal thicknesses. A loop is formed with the thicker cord and the thinner cord is threaded through the loop. The end is then taken round the doubled cord, and back under the thinner cord. The knot is tightened by pulling on the thinner cord with its ends together.

Upholsterer's slip knot (Fig 5)
This is the knot you will use most frequently and you should learn to tie it neatly and quickly. It is used for fastening twine, thread and cotton to begin a line of stitches or ties and is also used for tying in stuffings, putting in buttons, and for many other jobs. If, for example, you were fastening a button to button-back upholstery (such as on the headboard on page 62), this is how you would tie the twine ends protruding from the back hessian or board.

Hold the two ends of twine together between thumb and forefinger. The cord end on the right should be at least 10cm *(4in)* long from the finger and thumb (Fig 5a).

Take this end forward and up across the cords (Fig 5b).

Wind it twice round both cords and through the loop you have made (Fig 5c).

Pull on this cord to form a moderately tight knot (Fig 5d).

Now pull on the other cord to slip the knot up to the fabric surface at the required tension and give the shorter

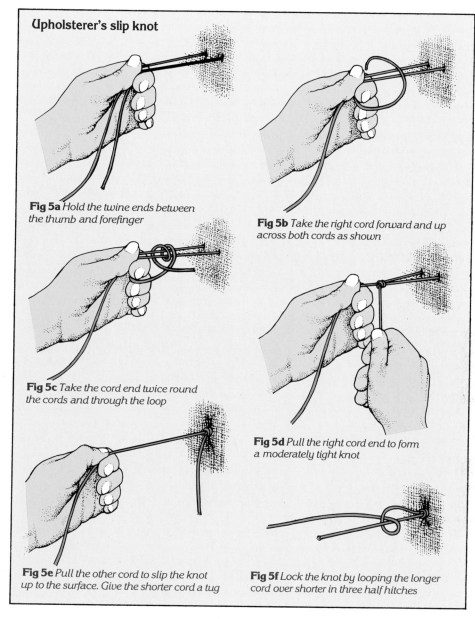

Upholsterer's slip knot

Fig 5a *Hold the twine ends between the thumb and forefinger*

Fig 5b *Take the right cord forward and up across both cords as shown*

Fig 5c *Take the cord end twice round the cords and through the loop*

Fig 5d *Pull the right cord end to form a moderately tight knot*

Fig 5e *Pull the other cord to slip the knot up to the surface. Give the shorter cord a tug*

Fig 5f *Lock the knot by looping the longer cord over shorter in three half hitches*

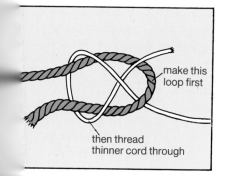

make this loop first

then thread thinner cord through

Sheet bend: *first form a loop with the cord, then thread the thinner cord with the loop, take round and tuck under. knot by pulling thin cord ends*

cord a tug to tighten the knot (Fig 5e).
6. Lock the knot by looping the longer cord over the shorter in three half hitches (Fig 5f).

Half hitch (Fig 6)
The half hitch forms part of several knots and can be used when joining on extra twine, or for joining on another length of thread.
1. Loop the new cord round the old short length (Fig 6a).
2. Slide it up to the last made stitch (Fig 6b).
3. Tie another half hitch, looping the new length over the old short end and pull tight (Fig 6c).

Do this two or three times so that it is secure and do not cut off the old end

too close to the knots - leave at least 2.5cm *(1in)*.

Lock loop (Fig 7)
This is used when lacing springs with laid cord and, as its name implies, is not really a knot but a loop that locks itself and it is easily adjustable (Fig 7).

Clove hitch (Fig 8)
Bring the cord over the spring from the back then take it under the coil, coming up on the right side of the cord.

Hold the cord between the thumb and index finger in a loop, then take the cord over the spring again, this time to the left and through the loop (Fig 8a).

Take away the finger and pull the knot tight (Fig 8b).

Joining on new twine

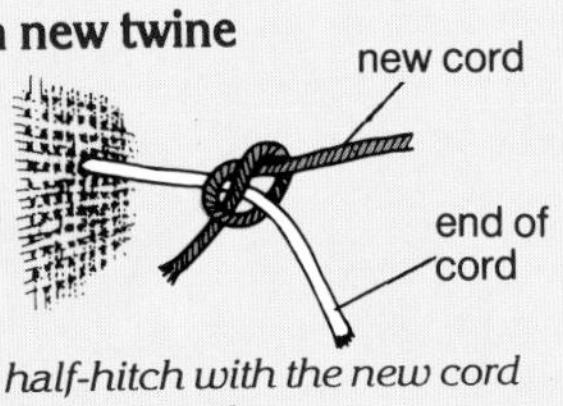

new cord

end of cord

Fig 6a *Tie a half-hitch with the new cord round the old short length*

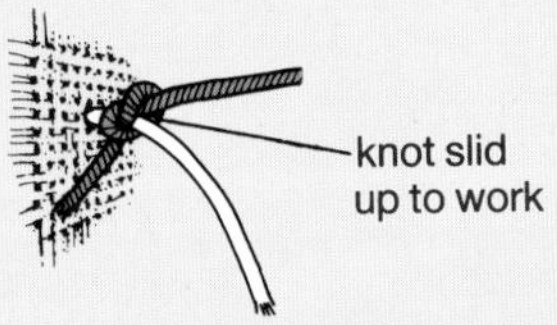

knot slid up to work

Fig 6b *Slide the knot up to the work as shown here*

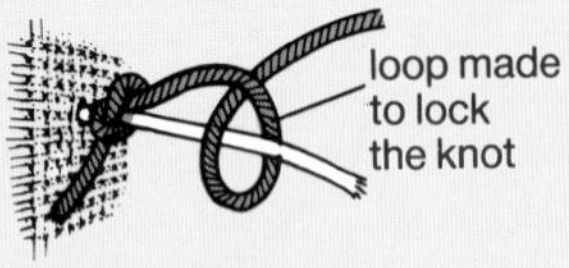

loop made to lock the knot

Fig 6c *Loop the new thread over the short end to lock*

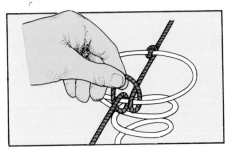

Fig 7 Lock loop: *bring the cord over the spring from the back, then under, coming up on the left side of the cord. Take it over the cord as illustrated and under the coil*

Fig 8a Clove hitch: *bring the cord over the spring from the back, then under, coming up on the right side. Hold the cord in a loop. Take it over the spring, to the left, and through the loop*

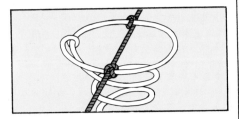

Fig 8b *Take the finger away and pull the clove hitch knot tight. These techniques are used to lace springs (see diagram 7, page 19)*

Basic Skills 3

Webbing is the next skill you need to master in the craft of upholstery and knowing how to do this in the right way is essential as the webbing forms the important basic support for the work that follows.

Fastening and lacing springs are also dealt with in this section.

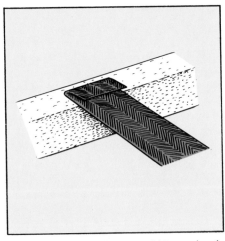

Fig 1 *Fold 2.5cm (1in) at the webbing end and place it on the chair rail*

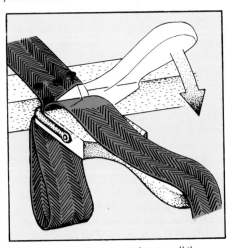

Fig 3 *Use the webbing stretcher to pull the webbing tight. Fasten with three tacks*

Webbing

Tools and materials required for this technique

Tools: scissors, hinged stirrup webbing stretcher, hammer. **Materials:** webbing, 16mm *(5/8in)* or 13mm *(1/2in)* improved tacks, PVA glue in a squeeze bottle.

1. Make a 2.5cm *(1in)* fold at the end of the webbing and place it on the frame with the fold uppermost (Fig 1).
2. Fix the webbing to the frame with a staggered row of tacks (Fig 2). Use your discretion as to the size and number of tacks. For most woods, four 16mm *(5/8in)* tacks will be about right but a very hard wood may need 13mm *(1/2in)* tacks. The heads should be level and flat with the surface.
3. Bring the other end of the webbing

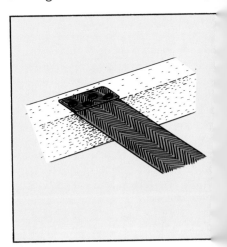

Fig 2 *Drive in four tacks in a staggered row through both thicknesses*

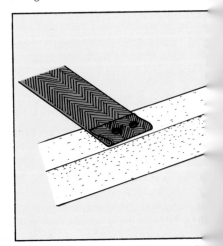

Fig 4 *Cut the webbing and fold it back. D a further two tacks between the first three*

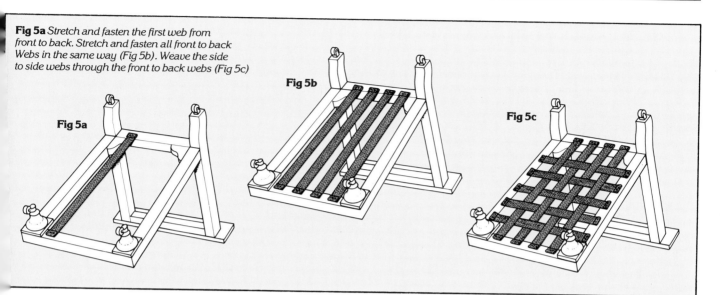

Fig 5a *Stretch and fasten the first web from front to back. Stretch and fasten all front to back Webs in the same way (Fig 5b). Weave the side to side webs through the front to back webs (Fig 5c)*

Fig 5a

Fig 5b

Fig 5c

cross the frame and slip on to the ebbing stretcher. Stretch the webbing bringing down the handle, then fix e webbing to the frame with three cks (Fig 3).

Cut off the webbing end 2.5cm *(1in)* m the tacks.

Fold up the end of the webbing and ve in another two tacks, positioning m between the first three (Fig 4).

acing webbing

gin by stretching and fixing the web m the back of the frame to the front g 5a). Fix the remaining webbing s from back to front (Fig 5b). he side to side webs are interwoven nd out (Fig 5c).

ome seat frames can present a lem in re-webbing – such as those pincushion seats where there is little width of wood. To give a better d to the fixing, squeeze a line of PVA along the frame where the bing is to be sited, then tack the ing down onto this.

rings

ize, gauge and number of springs varies according to the size and e of the seat to be upholstered, and egree of firmness required

ening springs

gs are first fastened to the ing support. No 1 stout twine is in a 12.5cm *(5in)* curved spring e. Start with an upholsterer's slip nd pass the needle through the ng, over the spring, and back

through the webbing. Make three of these fastening stitches, positioning them equidistantly round the spring base and knotting each stitch with a half hitch beneath the webbing. (Fig 6).

Springs are thus fastened through the heavy hessian spring covering.

Lacing springs

Having fastened the springs to the supporting webbing, the next stage is to lace them down with a laid cord. The diagram in Fig 7 illustrates a chair seat with five springs. Notice that six pieces of cord are used for lacing down.

To estimate the length required, stretch the cord over the springs from back to front, then add half the length again for knotting.

1. Tie a single knot in the end of each piece of cord and push a 16mm *(5/8in)* improved tack through the knots. Fasten three cords to the back rail in the centre of the wood and three cords to the left-hand rail. Position each cord so that it is centred on the springs. Hammer the tacks home.

2. Hold down the back, right hand spring about 5cm *(2in)* higher than the rails. Tie a lock loop on the back of the second coil and a clove hitch on the front of the top coil. This is to keep the springs straighter at the waist.

Bring the cord forward to the front right-hand spring. Tie a lock-loop on the top coil back. Then tie a clove hitch on the front of the second coil down.

Drive a tack half-way in on the front rail, then fasten the cord by twisting it round the tack. Adjust the tension, drive the tack home and tie a half-hitch to

secure. Take the cord end back to the top coil of the front spring. Pull fairly tight, then tie off with a clove hitch and a half hitch. Repeat with the other cords.

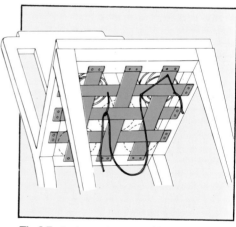

Fig 6 *Fastening springs to webbing: make three stitches round spring base, fastening with half hitches*

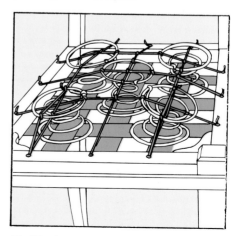

Fig 7 *Lacing springs: laid cords are stretched and knotted over springs from back to front, and from side to side*

Pincushion Seat Chair

This perhaps is the simplest form of upholstery and is therefore appropriate as a first project. Although the chair pictured on page 22 is a far from simple shape, once you have successfully coped with a curved serpentine seat, ordinary straight-sided pincushion seats will seem like child's play!

Preparation

Ripping off

1. First, pull off any old braid or trimming which will have been applied with glue. Remove the top fabric, lifting out any tacks.

On delicate frames such as the one pictured on page 22 where the wood is solid mahogany throughout, you will probably find that there is quite a lot of splitting and damage caused by the numerous tacks that have been used in the past. A ripping chisel and mallet could distress the frame even more, so employ the kinder method of removing the tacks with side-cutting pliers.

2. Remove the old layers of upholstery – taking note of them as you work. Under the top covering there will be a layer of wadding, then a calico covering over the horsehair or other filling. Tarpaulin hessian will be the final layer over the webbing.

Remove the webbing. Fill holes if this seems necessary.

Webbing up

3. The shape of this type of seat frame can cause slight problems when fastening the webbing, especially when trying to stretch it tightly. For a chair with a pronounced serpentine front, such as this, place a piece of rubber webbing along the outside of the front, holding the ends with a small 'G' clamp and wood blocks on each side rail so that the webbing stretcher can grip on the angle of the curve.

Fig 1 shows that four webs have been placed from the back to the front and then four more are interlaced from side to side. There is insufficient wood to attach the webbing properly so use a little glue beneath each web to give extra strength to the fastening. Then tack with 16mm (⅝in) fine tacks.

Basic Skills 4

Fastening hessian

Cut the hessian to shape and 2.5cm (1in) larger all round. Fold the allowance to the right side on one edge. Using 13mm (½in) improved tacks, tack the hessian to the frame through the doubled fabric, setting tacks about 3.5cm (1½in) apart (Fig 1). Stretch the hessian tightly and tack down the opposite side through a single thickness of fabric, setting tacks 5cm (2in) apart. Do the same on the two remaining sides, stretching the hessian smooth (Fig 2). Now turn the allowance over on the three sides and tack through the doubled fabric, setting tacks between those already underneath. Make sure the tacks are driven well home with the heads quite flat. If the wood tends to split easily, use finer tacks. In cases where the wood appears distressed by previous tack holes, glue can be used to assist in holding the hessian down and staples used instead of tacks, to avoid further damage to the wood.

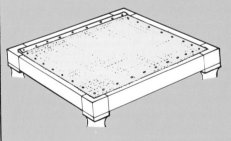

Fig 1 *Tack one side through the double thickness, then stretch and tack the other sides through a single thickness*

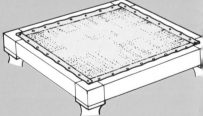

Fig 2 *Fold over the hessian allowance. Ta[ck] through double thickness on three sides*

Fastening tarpaulin hessian

4. For this chair, tarpaulin hessian, the thickest and strongest of upholstery hessians, is fastened over the webbing. (Refer to the techniques described in Basic Skills 4, and adapt them to y[our] particular chair seat.) Leave about (¼in) of bare wood between the hessian edge and the show wood f[or] subsequent tackings.

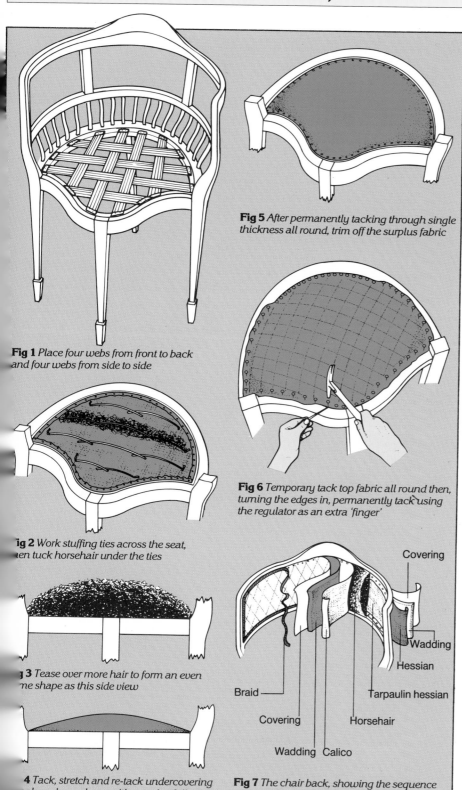

Fig 1 *Place four webs from front to back and four webs from side to side*

Fig 2 *Work stuffing ties across the seat, then tuck horsehair under the ties*

Fig 3 *Tease over more hair to form an even dome shape as this side view*

Fig 4 *Tack, stretch and re-tack undercovering to make a dome shape without edge fullness*

Fig 5 *After permanently tacking through single thickness all round, trim off the surplus fabric*

Fig 6 *Temporary tack top fabric all round then, turning the edges in, permanently tack using the regulator as an extra 'finger'*

Fig 7 *The chair back, showing the sequence of layers forming the upholstery*

Covering

Wadding

Hessian

Tarpaulin hessian

Horsehair

Calico

Wadding

Covering

Braid

Tools and materials required for this project

Tools: side-cutting pliers, hole filler, webbing stretcher, G clamps and wooden blocks, glue, hammer, scissors, trimming scissors, cabriole hammer, regulator. **Materials:** webbing, tarpaulin hessian, No. 2 or No. 3 twine and curved needle, horsehair stuffing, unbleached calico, cotton wadding, top fabric, braid, 10mm (³⁄₈in) fine tacks, 13mm (¹⁄₂in) improved tacks, 16mm (⁵⁄₈in) fine tacks.

Basic skills used in this project

Ripping off – page 16
Webbing – page 18
Fastening hessian – page 20
Stuffing ties – page 21
Stuffing – page 21
Applying undercovering – page 21
Applying cotton wadding – page 23
Applying top covering – page 23
Applying trimming – page 24

Stuffing

6. For the best and most lasting results, use good quality horsehair stuffing. Tuck lines of stuffing under the ties (as shown in Fig 2). If the lines of hair are placed evenly and are of uniform density and size, the even distribution of stuffing over the seat will be assured.
7. The next step is to fill in between the lines of hair. Tease over a further layer of hair to form a dome shape as shown in Fig 4.

The amount of stuffing required will depend on the quality of the horsehair. Shorter horsehair consolidates under pressure, while the better quality, long-stranded variety will stay high and springy until it is confined by the undercovering.

Undercovering

8. At this point, the mass of horsehair must be pulled down and contained with an undercovering of strong, unbleached calico. Roughly measure the size of calico required and tear the fabric. (Tearing rather than cutting ensures that the piece is on the straight grain.) This undercovering is put in place with temporary tacking, where tacks are driven only part way in. This means that they can be removed easily

Stuffing ties

To anchor the stuffing in place, stuffing ties in the form of large stitches are to be put into the hessian in lines across the seat.

Use No. 2 or No. 3 twine and the curved needle, and, beginning with an upholsterer's slip knot, work the stitches as shown in Fig 2, finishing with two half hitches.

The ties (or loops) should be just gently tight.

Project One

*Late nineteenth-century
pincushion seat chair
covered in figured damask*

and the covering re-adjusted and re-tacked accordingly.

9. Use 10mm *(³⁄₈in)* fine tacks. Begin by placing one tack in the centre of the back rail, one in the centre of the front rail and one in the centre of each side. Make sure the tacks are placed inside the polished show wood.

10. Insert more tacks partway along the back rail at intervals of 4cm *(1¹⁄₂in)*. Do the same along the front and then down the sides until the entire seat is surrounded with tacks.

11. Now you can begin to adjust and tighten the calico by removing three or four tacks from the centre back and stretching the calico a little before re-tacking again temporarily. Continue this treatment all round the rails, taking out tacks, stretching the calico and then re-tacking.

Pay particular attention to the diagonal stretching of the undercovering as this will help to produce a beautifully-rounded dome shape without any edge fullness to the seat.

12. When a pleasing and even shape has been achieved, drive home all the tacks, making sure that they are at a distance of at least 3mm *(¹⁄₈in)* in from the show wood's edge (Fig 4).

There is no need to turn under the calico, as tacking through the single thickness is quite sufficient. Trim off the surplus fabric all round (Fig 5).

Cotton wadding

Horsehair will work its way through loosely-woven fabrics and, to prevent this happening, the calico is overlaid with two layers of cotton wadding. Spread the wadding and trim the edges to the line of tacks.

Top covering

This is the stage all home upholsterers look forward to – putting on the covering fabric.

Mark the centre of the front of the seat on the calico edge using a soft pencil. Mark the centre of the back of the seat. Measure the seat and cut a piece of covering material that is 25mm larger all round.

Mark the centres of the front and back edges by folding lengthways and snipping the fold to make a small V. Make sure that the wadding is lying smoothly and is crease-free, then lay the covering over and position it so

One of the two piped seams that are made on the inside covering to eliminate fullness on the curved back of the pincushion seat chair

The outside back covered with the fabric and then trimmed with matching braid. Note the neatly mitred corner

that the V snips correspond with the marks on the centre front and centre back of the calico. Temporarily tack, in the same way as when putting on the undercover, but this time taking care to keep the weave (straight grain) absolutely straight, from back to front and from side to side.

16. Using a cabriole hammer, work the temporary tacks all round using 10mm *(³⁄₈in)* fine tacks (or gimp pins if the wood tends to split) and inserting the tacks at intervals of 3cm *(1¹⁄₄in)*. Tension the fabric just enough to take out its natural elasticity (but remember that the seat has already been tensioned with the calico undercovering).

17. Trim the fabric to shape all round leaving 13mm *(¹⁄₂in)* for turning in. You are now ready to permanently fasten.

18. Remove three or four tacks from the centre back, fold under the excess fabric and drive the tacks fully home.

Use a cabriole hammer with a very small head to drive in the tacks to avoid damaging the surrounding wood. After fastening partway along the back edge, you can turn your attention to the front edge and work here, starting at the centre and working outwards towards the corners (Fig 6). Work the remaining parts of the sides by working back from the front corners.

Fig 6 shows that the regulator is used as a 'finger' when the edges of the fabric are being turned in. The fabric can be given a little stretch and then held in place with the regulator while the tack is driven home. A neater and more accurate job can be done in this way than if you try and hold the fabric with just a finger.

Chair back

19. Fig 7 shows the sequence of layers forming the complete upholstery.

There is no webbing in the back but stout tarpaulin hessian is stretched tightly over the inside back as the basic support for the upholstery. This is stretched mostly from bottom to top and very little from side to side, thus preserving the inward-curving shape.

20. Work two rows of stuffing ties round the inside back and place a thin, light layer of horsehair under the ties. This must not be too thick or you will have difficulty in eliminating fullness in the covering fabric. Use no more than 3cm *(1¹⁄₄in)* depth of loosely-teased hair.

21. The tight calico undercover goes on next, temporarily tacked, adjusted, permanently tacked and then trimmed round. Place the cotton wadding on next and then the top covering can be put on.

22. When putting on the undercover and the top covering, begin tacking (both temporary and permanent) from the bottom and top centres and working out to the sides. Concentrate on tightening from bottom to top, stretching sideways only enough to eliminate any fullness that may remain.

Covering the outside back

23. This is just a simple matter of stretching a piece of strong but lighter-weight hessian over the back. Over this, lay cotton wadding, then finish off with the covering fabric.

Trim the seat and the inside and outside of the chair back with braid (see page 24).

Basic Skills 5

Applying trimmings

There are a number of adhesives which can be used for fastening braid trimmings but be wary of those which are latex-based because if any of the glue gets onto the covering fabric it is almost impossible to remove. The adhesive used by many professional upholsterers is a thixotropic impact adhesive. This is jelly-like and is easily spread with a blade. It sticks tightly only when firmly pressed down, which allows for some adjustment in fitting the braid.

Applying braid

1. Secure the braid end to the chair, right sides facing, with two gimp pins (Fig 1). This is called back-tacking.
2. Apply a thin line of adhesive to the fabric (Fig 2).
3. Hold the braid end and spread adhesive thinly along it, coating only enough of the braid to trim one side of the chair at a time. Scrape the glue along to ensure an even, thin application. Stretch the braid along the chair side, gently pressing it down with the fingers (Fig 3).
4. To finish off, cut the braid end 6mm (¼in) longer than needed and fold under (Fig 4). Apply a little adhesive to the underside and press in position. Leave to set for about five minutes, then roll along the braid with a seam roller.

Decorative cord trims the pouffe (page 31) and is sewn into a looped knot at all four corners.

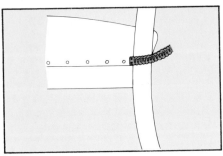

Fig 1 *Starting at the back upright, secure the braid end with gimp pins*

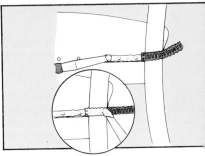

Fig 2 *Spread adhesive very thinly along the fabric edge then along the braid itself, slightly stretching it*

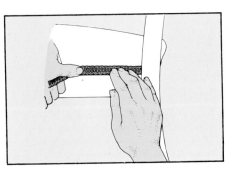

Fig 3 *Hold the braid end in one hand and stretch it along the fabric, pressing gently into place*

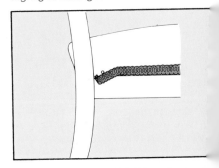

Fig 4 *Cut the braid end, fold it under, spread a little glue on it, and press into position*

Fig 5 *Catch the braid loops to the fabric*

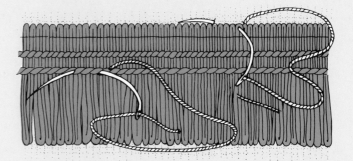

Fig 6 *Fix fringe to fabric with two rows of stitches*

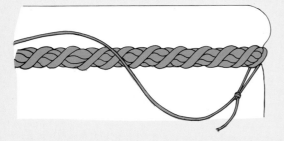

Fig 7 *Sewing on cord: begin with a slip knot*

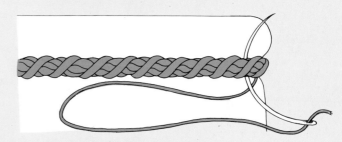

Fig 8 *Make a stitch through the cord centre*

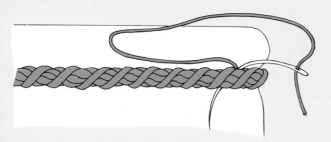

Fig 9 *Go back a fraction, making a stitch beneath the cord*

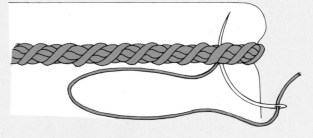

Fig 10 *Go back a fraction, making a stitch at 90 degrees through centre of cord*

Sewing braids, fringes and cords

You should not rely on adhesive alone for fastening braid because, after a year or two, it deteriorates and comes apart from the chair easily. Always sew braid after glueing for extra security.

Sewing on braid

Using a curved needle and matching sewing thread, catch the top loops of the braid to the fabric underneath (Fig 5). Use very small stitches so that they cannot be seen.

Sewing on fringe

Glue is not used for attaching fringing. In Fig 6, two rows of stitches are illustrated, the first along the top edge, taking the curved needle through the loops and then into the fabric. The stitches on the lower edge of the fringe are like small running stitches.

Sewing on decorative cords

This type of trimming always sets off a chair well, giving a very luxurious look. Chair cord is a silken twisted cord, usually 6–9mm (*1/4–3/8in*) in diameter.

First, ladder stitch the seams where the cord is to be used – usually the arm scrolls, the front border, the wings and, perhaps, the top of the outside back.

Pin the cord in position over the seams and sew with a fine 7.5cm (*3in*)-long, 19 gauge curved cording needle.
1. Begin with a small stitch and a slip knot which will be hidden under the cord (Fig 7). Make a stitch through the centre of the cord (Fig 8).
2. Reinsert the needle a fraction back from where it came out and pass the needle into the fabric and in line with the seam. Bring the needle out on the lower edge of the cord (Fig 9).
3. Reinsert the needle a fraction back from the last stitch and make a stitch through the centre of the cord at 90 degrees (Fig 10).

Continue along the cord in the same way to the end.

To finish, estimate where the cord will end, allow sufficient to turn under the end (about 13mm (*1/2in*)) and then wrap the end with transparent adhesive tape. Cut the cord through the tape to prevent ravelling. Tuck in and sew in place.

Drop-in Seat Chair

This type of seat is a separate, removable upholstered seat frame which fits into the seat rails. This is an ideal project for a beginner because it uses many of the basic upholstery skills. In this project, you will learn how to handle undercovering and achieve a smooth even surface and also how to make the neat tailored corners that will give your work the truly professional look that is the ideal.

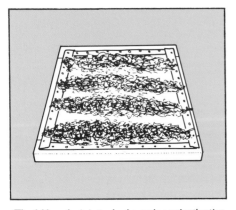

Fig 1 *The seat frame, showing the spacing of the webbing, three front to back, three side to side*

Fig 2 *Stretch the hessian over the webbing. Set front frame tacks through double thickness*

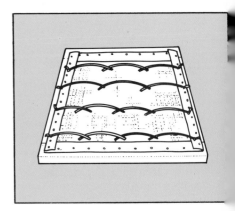

Fig 3 *Work four lines filling ties across the sea They should be taut but not tight*

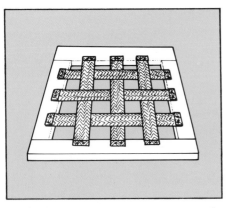

Fig 4 *Horsehair is tucked evenly under the ties. Next fill in evenly between the lines*

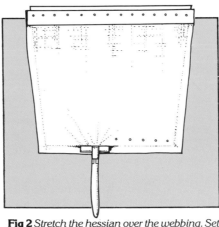

Fig 5 *Tease over a further layer to form a dome of filling. Here it is viewed from side*

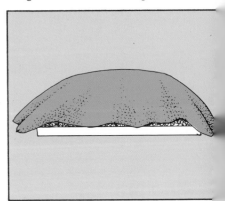

Fig 6 *Place the undercovering over the filling that it hangs equally on all four sides*

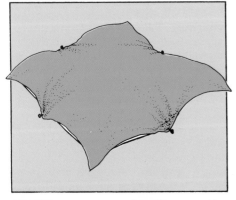

Fig 7 *Place temporary tacks at the centre sides, just enough to hold the fabric in place*

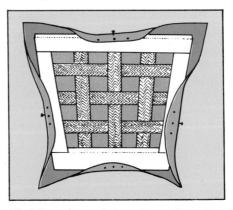

Fig 8 *Temporary tack the undercovering to the rails, driving three tacks into the centre of each side*

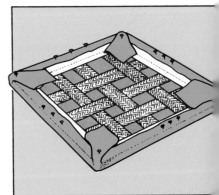

Fig 9 *Fold the corners and then temporary them to secure as shown here*

Tools and materials required for this project
Tools: ripping chisel and mallet, scissors, small trimmers, webbing stretcher, claw hammer. **Materials:** webbing, horsehair, calico, cotton wadding, tarpaulin hessian, top fabric, 13mm *(1/2in)* fine tacks, 10mm *(3/8in)* fine tacks, 12.5cm *(5in)* curved needle, and No. 2 and No. 3 twine.

Basic Skills used in this project

...arver chair which has seen many ...rations, such as new arms and seat rails. ...s been upholstered in tapestry

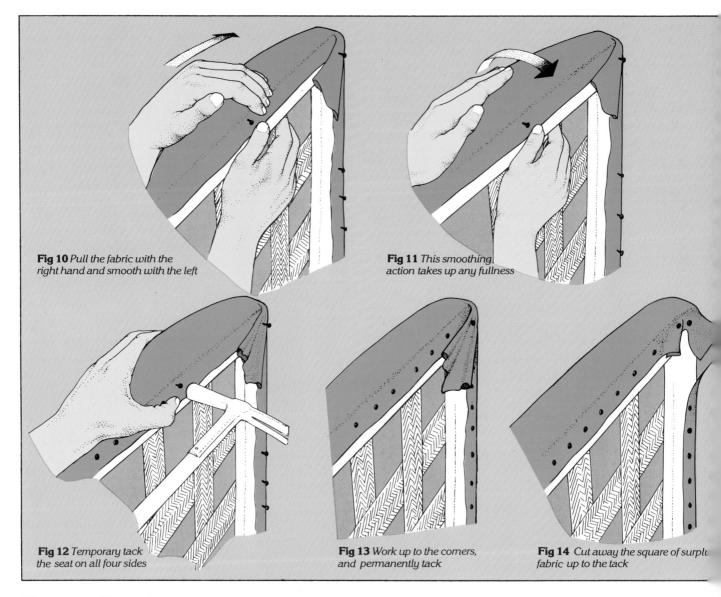

Fig 10 *Pull the fabric with the right hand and smooth with the left*

Fig 11 *This smoothing action takes up any fullness*

Fig 12 *Temporary tack the seat on all four sides*

Fig 13 *Work up to the corners, and permanently tack*

Fig 14 *Cut away the square of surplus fabric up to the tack*

Preparation

Measuring up
1. Before stripping the piece, measure the seat from back to front and from side to side at the widest points, allowing about 5cm *(2in)* extra all round for turnings.

Ripping off
2. Remove the old layers of upholstery and filling, taking note of the arrangement of the original webbing. Remove tacks and fill holes where necessary.

When the frame is bare, examine the joints to make sure they are sound and re-glue any if necessary.

Check the fit of the frame in the chair. If a thicker fabric than before is going to

be used, it may be necessary to plane some wood from the seat frame.

Webbing up
3. Fasten the new webbing (Fig 1). Stretch and fasten tarpaulin hessian over the webbing (Fig 2). Refer to page 26.

Stuffing ties
4. Using No. 2 or No. 3 twine in a 12.5cm *(5in)* curved needle, work stuffing ties across the seat, beginning with an upholsterer's slip knot and ending with two half hitches. The ties should be fairly taut but not too tight (see Fig 3, page 26).

Stuffing
5. Tuck lines of horsehair filling evenly under the ties (Fig 4). Then fill in evenly between the lines. Tease over a further

layer of stuffing to form a dome-like mass as shown in Fig 5, page 26.

Undercovering
6. Tear a piece of calico to the size required and lay it loosely over the stuffing so that the fabric hangs equally on all four sides (Fig. 6). Drive temporary tacks (use 13mm *(½in)* fine tacks), into the centre of each side, just enough to hold the fabric (Fig 7).
7. Hold the seat so that the back edge is on the work surface and the left edge towards you. Drive three temporary tacks into the centre of each rail on the underside (Fig 8).
8. Now gently stretch the fabric at the corners, pulling it diagonally. This gives the seat an even, domed shape. Keep a check on the straight grain of the fabric threads in the middle of the seat. If th

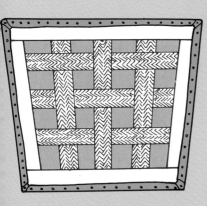

Fig 15 *Permanently tack all round keeping within 13mm (1/2in) of the edge. Trim off surplus calico*

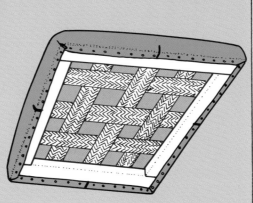

Fig 16 *Mark the side centres of the top covering on the edges and underneath*

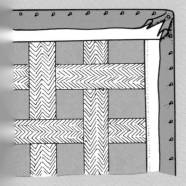

Fig 17 *Tack the corners and cut away surplus cloth as you did for the undercover (see Fig 14)*

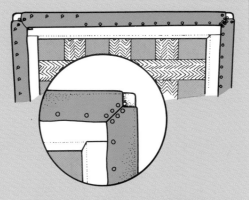

Fig 18 *Turn the fabric edges under and tack, removing temporary tacks. Pleat and tack corners as detail*

reads are not exactly straight from
ck to front and from side to side, you
e stretching too far on one corner or
other.

Fold the fabric at the corners (see Fig
and place temporary tacks to hold
e corners.

Still holding the seat on its edge, take
t the temporary tacks in the centre of
front edge. (Tuck back any stuffing
t has worked its way over the edge of
wood.) Hold the seat as shown in
10. Pull the fabric with the right
nd while you smooth and compress
stuffing with the left. As the fabric is
usted, place a temporary tack in the
tre of the edge (see Fig 10).

orking away from you, smooth and
tch the fabric along the front of the
t (Fig 11). This action takes up any
ess and eliminates the possibility of

tack marks (lines in the fabric which run
from the tack). This can occur only if
the fabric is pulled very tightly at the
point where it is held by the tack while
remaining looser between tacks.

Do not pull on the fabric – just hold it
while you smooth and gently stretch it
to take up any slack. On the last
smoothing stroke of the left hand, bring
the thumb over and hold the fabric
while you pick up the tack and hammer.
Hammer in the tack to secure the fabric
temporarily (Fig 12).

10. Repeat this procedure on the other
three sides of the seat. Then continue
adding temporary tacks on each side of
the central tacks, working towards the
corners (Fig 12).

The last tacks should be 7cm (2¾in)
from the corners (Fig 13).

Take out the temporary tacks at the

corners and, pulling the corners down
again, drive a tack home at each corner
(Fig 13). Cut away a square of surplus
fabric up to the tack.

Corners

11. Continue the stretching process
right up to the corners, pleating the
corners as shown in Fig 14. Now
permanently tack with 10mm (³/8in)
fine tacks all round the seat (Fig 15),
keeping within 13mm (1/2in) of the
outside edge.

Remove the temporary tacks and
trim off the surplus calico.

The seat should now have an even
shape but you may notice that
horsehair is working its way through the
fabric. To arrest its progress, cotton
wadding is now placed on top.

Wadding

12. Cut two layers of wadding and lay
them on the undercover. Trim the
edges so that none of it extends over
the sides (remember that the seat has
to fit into the chair frame).

Top covering

13. Cut the top fabric to size and fold in
half and then in half again to find the
centre. Snip notches into the edges of
the folds so that the middle of all four
sides is marked. Measure and mark the
middle of the seat sides with a soft
pencil taking the line over to the
underside (Fig 16).

14. Lay the fabric over the seat
matching the marks and notches. If,
because of the shape of the seat, the
marks at the sides of the seat do not
match the fabric, make sure that they are
the same distance apart on each side.

Temporary tack, taking extra care to
ensure that the straight grain of the
fabric is true.

Corners (top fabric)

15. The corners must be pleated neatly.
Permanently fix a tack in each corner
(Fig 17) and cut away the fabric up to
the tack as you did for the undercover.
Fold the edges of the corners in and
permanently tack (see Fig 18).

Finishing

16. Turn the edges under all round and
permanently tack, removing the
temporary tacks as you work (Fig 18).
Note the method used for finishing the
corners, shown in the detail.

Stuffed Pouffe

This is a most useful and versatile piece of furniture providing extra seating when required, or a flat surface at exactly the right height for board games. Covered in a rich-looking fabric, a pouffe makes a sumptuous and elegant addition to a family room. If you have the use of a sewing machine, you will find this a very easy project.

Preparation

Making the inner case
1. First determine the size and shape of the pouffe required. The average size is about 35cm *(15in)* square and 28cm *(11in)* high. Fig 1 shows that the inner case is simply a box-shaped fabric bag with four sides, a top and a bottom piece.

For a 38cm *(15in)*-square pouffe you will need a top and bottom panel cut to this size plus 13mm *(½in)* all round for seam allowances.

Cut the side panel in one piece 155cm *(61in)* long by the depth of the pouffe (28cm *(11in)*) plus 2.5cm *(1in)* for seam allowances.
2. Place the top and bottom panels together and pin them. Snip V's into the edges (these V-marks will help you later in fitting the top and bottom panels to the side panel). Remove the pins.

Stitching
3. Right sides facing, pin the top panel to the side panel, setting pins across the seam. Machine-stitch all round (Fig 2). When you reach the open corner, stitch

this in one with the seam.
4. With the top panel in position, follow the grain of the side panel fabric to mark V's on the bottom edge to match up with the V's on the bottom panel edges. If the fabric is too finely woven to see the grain, you may need to pull a thread to ascertain the straight grain.
5. With right sides facing, machine-stitch the bottom panel to the side panel, leaving a gap in the seam for a stuffing mouth. Turn the inner case to the right side through the gap, ready for stuffing.

Stuffing the pouffe
6. The stuffing must be well-teased before filling the case with it. Put a few handfuls into the case and, keeping the top side flat on the work surface, distribute it evenly and compress it down over the bottom of the case. (The pouffe is set this way, top side down, so that a smooth, flat surface is achieved in the finished pouffe.)
7. Add layers in the same way, compressing it with your hand until the case is firmly stuffed.

Finishing the inner case
8. Close the filling mouth with skewers and, to consolidate the stuffing even more, sit on the case and bounce up and down.
You will probably find that more stuffing can now be added.

Take care that the shape is kept square and that the sides do not bulge.
9. Ladder-stitch the filling mouth, using the 17 gauge curved needle and strong thread, to close it.

Shaping the pouffe
10. With a length of stout twine, tie the 'waist' of the pouffe tightly, using an upholsterer's slip knot (see Fig 3).

Insulating
11. If short horsehair has been used for the filling, wrap the entire case with a layer of cotton wadding. If any other filling has been used, surround this with a layer of bonded polyester wadding, fastening it with large stitches to make a complete covering 'skin'. Use a stout sewing thread in the 10cm *(4in)*

Fig 1 *The pouffe inner case consists of a top and bottom piece, plus a side panel cut in one piece. V's are snipped in the edges*

Fig 2 *Machine-stitch the top piece to the side panel piece. The open seam of the side panel is stitched in one with the seam*

Fig 3 *With the pouffe upside down fill throu*ɡ *the seam, then sew it up with Ladder-stitchi*ɡ *then tie the waist with twine*

Tools and material used in this project

Tools: ruler, shears, trimming scissors, sewing machine, upholsterer's pins, 7.5cm *(3in)* 17 gauge and 7.5cm *(3in)* 19 gauge and 10cm *(4in)* 16 gauge curved needles, thread, 10cm *(4in)* skewer, regulator. **Materials:** calico or ticking, stuffing (short horsehair, coconut fibre or carded sisal), polyester and cotton wadding, top fabric, trimmings.

Basic skills used in this project

Machine-stitching — page 30
Stuffing — page 21
Applying trimming — page 24

curved needle. Tie the 'waist' of the pouffe again, to recover its shape.

Outer cover

12. Make up the outer cover in the same way as the inner case except for the bottom panel which should be stitched to the side panel on one edge only to enable the cover to be slipped on easily. Neaten all seam allowances with zigzag machine-stitches or oversewing by hand.

13. Slip the cover onto the pouffe and finish the open seams with ladder stitching.

Note: Generally, covers are made to the same size as the inner case but if the covering fabric has very little stretch, it may be necessary to make it larger than the inner case so that the cover slips on easily. The bottom panel can be made of a more substantial fabric such as thick cotton platform fabric or leather cloth but if the pouffe is to stand on soft, clean carpet then it can be made reversible with the top and bottom fabrics the same.

Trimming

14. There are several ways in which a pouffe can be trimmed. The top and bottom seams can be piped, or ready-made ruching can be inserted into the seams when the cover is being made up.

A stout, decorative cord has been used to trim the pouffe in the picture. Measure round the pouffe and cut the cord to the measurement plus 2.5cm *(1in)*. (Before cutting the cord, wind self-adhesive tape round the cord and cut through the tape and cord to prevent the ends unravelling.) With the regulator, open up a hole in the seam, without disturbing the stitches and push the end of the cord into the hole.

Attach the cord by sewing as described on page 25, then push the other end of the cord into the same hole in the seam.

Ready-made cord with tassels can be purchased as curtain tie-backs and these can be adapted for the waist trimming. Sew the waist cord in position. If this type of cord is not available, use the top and bottom trimming cord doubled and finish the ends with neat loops, at the corners. Conceal the cut ends by tucking them into holes made in the seams.

Basic Skills 6

Close-nailing

Close-nailing is a method of trimming and permanently fastening down fabric with a row of dome-headed chair nails. Always choose the best quality available, with brass domes and steel shanks, for a lasting finish. Different sizes of chair nails can be obtained but the size most commonly used in upholstery has a 13mm *(¹⁄₂in)* shank with a 10mm *(³⁄₈in)* diameter head. Three finishes are available: polished brass, and dark and light antique finish. Choose one which closely matches your upholstery.

Close-nailing has the disadvantage that the rows of shanks tends to perforate wood along the grain. Some such as oak, may split along this line.

Beginner's gauge

Professional upholsterers nail by eye and, with practice, you will be able to do this, too. For now, a simple, handmade gauge will help you to achieve a professional effect. If you are unaccustomed to working with metal, have a handyman make the gauge for you.

You will need a 12.5cm *(5in)*-long strip of aluminium about 3mm *(¹⁄₈in)* thick and to a width the exact diameter of the nail head (Fig 1).

File a slot in the bottom to fit the nail's shank. The length of the slot should equal the radius of the nail's head. Bend the strip as shown in Fig 2.

To use the gauge, place it against the edge of the show wood (or level with the bottom of the seat rail).

Place the nail in the slot and drive it almost home.

Slip the gauge from the nail and complete driving home the nail.

Place the gauge close up against the nail head to position the next nail. When this is driven in the heads should just touch.

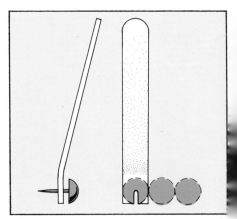

Fig 1 *A simple gauge made for close-nailing*

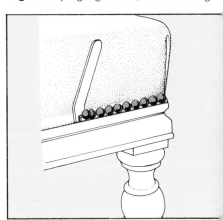

Fig 2 *To use the gauge place it against the edge of the show wood as demonstrated here*

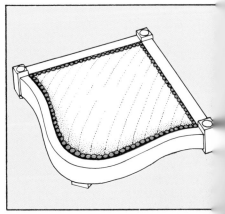

Fig 3 *A close-nailed chair seat edge, the chair nails both trimming and fastening the fabric*

...ghteenth-century-style armchair covered in ...amask and trimmed with 'antique' brass chair ...ails.

Stuffed-over Seat

The term 'stuffed-over' describes an upholstered chair seat which is built permanently onto the chair frame. Upholstering a dining room chair of this type is an extremely good project for a beginner because it includes almost all the basic skills of traditional upholstery. Once you have succeeded in upholstering a stuffed-over chair such as the one pictured, you will feel confident enough to tackle more complicated projects.

Preparation

The chair pictured is a simple, straight-edged chair without springs.

1. Remove all the old upholstery and tacks.
2. Fasten webbing to the rails and, as the seat is fairly wide, place four pieces of webbing each way. Fasten tarpaulin hessian over the webbing.

Stuffing ties

3. Put in the stuffing ties about 2.5cm (1in) from the frame edge all the way round (Fig 1).
4. Tuck stuffing under the loops of twine to form a wall all round the seat (see Fig 2a). In Fig 2b, you will see the shape to aim for. Corners are difficult to work but try and make them as firm as the rest of the edge. This can be done by rolling in extra hair and binding this on to the hair already held by the ties.

Make the wall about 1cm (³⁄8in) higher than you intend the finished seat to be, and extend it so that it overhangs the rails by about 2cm (³⁄4in).
5. Now fill up the centre with hair to form a domed shape.

Covering the stuffing

6. Measure and cut a piece of scrim allowing 2.5cm (1in) all round for turnings.

Mark the front and back edges of the scrim in the middle. Measure and mark the middle of the chair front and the back rails.
7. Lay the scrim over the stuffing and position it, matching marks. Temporary tack (Fig 3, page 36).
8. Check that the scrim weave is straight and cut into the back corners as shown in Fig 3 to within 1cm (³⁄8in) of the back uprights.
9. Turn the scrim over, cut off the surplus fabric and, using the regulator, tuck in the remainder (Fig 4).
10. Put in temporary tacks all the way round the seat, adjusting the covering until the shape is satisfactory.
11. Turn under the scrim edge and fasten it permanently along the tacking chamfer on the frame edge, placing tacks no more than 2cm (³⁄4in) apart. At the front and the back, align the tacks along a thread of the scrim. These edges of the seat should be of the same height and parallel to each other.
12. Now work the corners. Tack the

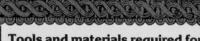

Tools and materials required for this project

Tools: ripping chisel and mallet, sharp knife and scissors, webbing stretcher, heavy and lightweight hammers, 10cm (4in) and 12.5cm (5in) curved needles, 25cm (10in) double-pointed needle, regulator, upholstery gauge and felt-tipped pen, 16mm (⁵⁄8in) improved tacks, 13mm (¹⁄2in) improved tacks, 10mm (³⁄8in) fine tacks, gimp pins, No. 1 and No. 3 twine. **Materials:** medium-thickness cardboard, webbing, tarpaulin hessian, horsehair, scrim, calico, wadding, top covering, trimming and adhesive.

Basic skills used in this project

Ripping off — page 16
Webbing — page 18
Fastening hessian — page 20
Stuffing ties — page 21
Edge-stitching and roll edges — page 3
Top stuffing — page 21
Applying undercovering — page 21
Applying top covering — page 23
Applying trimming — page 24

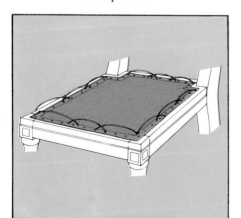

Fig 1 *Put in stuffing ties all round the seat setting them about 2.5cm (1in) from the frame edge*

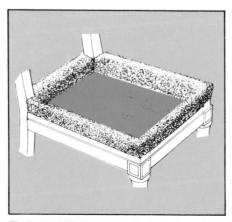

Fig 2a *Tuck stuffing under the twine loops to form a wall like this. Aim for a firm edge and corners*

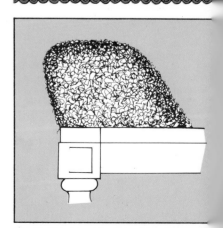

Fig 2b *This is a side view of the shape you should try and achieve. Keep corners firm*

centre of each corner, then make a small pleat on each side. (You will probably have to make several attempts to get this exactly right.) The corners must all be the same height and have the same overhang. Put in little more stuffing at this point if it seems necessary.

Using the regulator

13. At this state, the regulator is used to redistribute the stuffing as required. If there appears to be a lump – or a hollow – in the stuffing, push the regulator in about a third of its length

and, keeping the fulcrum where the regulator enters the surface, lever the filling into the hollow – or away from it – as required.

Through stuffing ties

14. Through stuffing ties are used to anchor the top scrim through the stuffing into the hessian and webbing underneath.

With a felt-tipped pen and the upholstery gauge, mark the surface of the scrim with a square, the edges about 10cm (4in) in from the sides.

15. Take a 25cm (10in)-long doubl pointed needle and No. 1 stout twin the back, right hand corner of the square, make a stitch about 16mm (⅝in) long, taking it through the se Tie the stitch loosely with an upholsterer's slip knot. Work stitche shown in Fig 5, finishing with a stitc the middle of the seat.

16. Pull down the ties tightly, holdin the slack as you do so, with each tie turn, starting with the first slip knot a ending with the centre stitch. Faster with a number of half hitches.

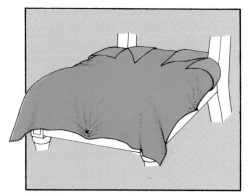

Fig 3 *Temporary-tack the scrim then cut into the back corners to within 1cm (⅜in) of the back uprights*

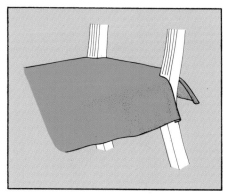

Fig 4 *Cut off the surplus fabric and tuck in the remainder. Use the regulator to do this*

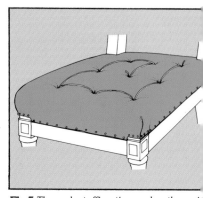

Fig 5 *Through stuffing ties anchor the scri the hessian and webbing. Finish in the mi of the seat*

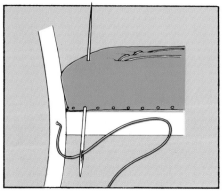

Fig 6a *Edge stitching: push the needle in about 3cm (1¼in) from the left hand corner*

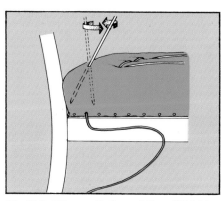

Fig 6b *Pull the needle through 9cm (3½in) in from the edge, twist it anti-clockwise*

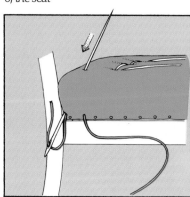

Fig 6c *Push the needle back so that it eme at the far end of the corner, on the line of ta*

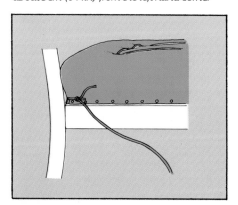

Fig 6d *Pull the twine through and tie with an upholsterer's slip knot, pulled tightly*

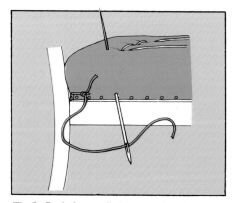

Fig 6e *Push the needle in again 4cm (1½in) to right of knot at the angle shown*

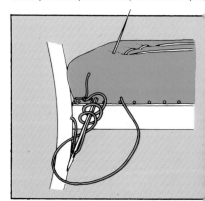

Fig 6f *Take twine three times round the ne clockwise. Pull needle out to tighten stitch*

ge-stitching

ge-stitching is worked with 'blind'
ches to bind the stuffing into a dense
on the chair edges, making it firm
ugh to be sat upon and keep its
pe. To start edge-stitching, you will
d a 25cm *(10in)* double-pointed
dle and about 3m *(3¼yd)* of No. 3
e. Blind stitches are worked from
to right. Start at the front left hand
ner.

Begin by pushing in the needle as
se as possible to the line of tacks
ut 3cm *(1¼in)* from the back
ight. Bring the point out above,
ut 9cm *(3½in)* in from the edge
6a).

Pull the needle through as far as its
Give the needle a twist in an anti-
ckwise direction to 'scoop' the
sehair inside the seat with the eye-
point of the needle (Fig 6b).
Push the needle back so that it
erges at the far end of the corner
se to the back upright), again just
he line of tacks (the needle point
uld actually scrape the wood)
6c).

Pull through and tie with an
olsterer's slip knot. Pull tightly
6d).

ush the needle in again 4cm
in) to the right of the knot at the
e shown (Fig 6e). Do the 'scoop'
on again and return the needle so
half its length comes out in front of
re the last stitch ended. Now take
twine and wind it clockwise round
needle, three times (Fig 6f).

Pull the needle and twine right out
tighten the stitch just made.
Continue across the chair in the
e way, working the back last.
Work another row of 'blind' stitches
e same way, 10–13mm *(³⁄₈–½in)*
ve the first row, on the front, right
left sides but not at the back as one
is worked across there.

king a roll

A roll is worked round the seat edge
ive sharpness of form when it is
ered. The method used is similar to
d' stitching but differs in that the
hes go through to the top surface.
re starting, use the regulator again
ring up the edge and deal with any
py or soft places.

Using the upholstery gauge and a
ipped pen, mark a line 23mm
n) in from the top surface edge and

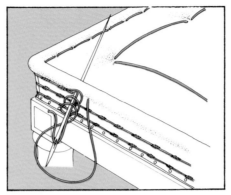

Fig 7a *Wind the twine three times round the needle as for edge stitches and pull up very tightly*

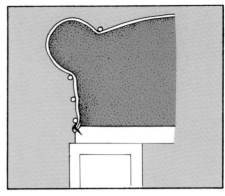

Fig 7b *This is the firm, roll edge you are working to achieve shown as a side view in plan*

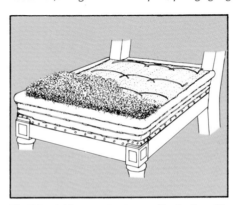

Fig 8 *Tuck filling under the ties, 'feathering off' a little at the roll edge*

Fig 9 *Cut cardboard stiffeners to shape and tack them round the corners*

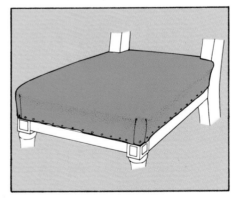

Fig 10 *The undercovering of calico brings the seat to its finished shape. Tack it down with no turnings*

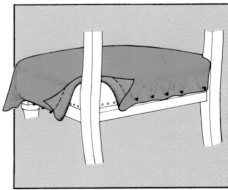

Fig 11 *Cut the corners to within 6mm (¼in) of the wood, stretch and temporarily tack*

then mark another just above the top
row of 'blind' stitches on the sides.
26. First, work a single stitch at the right
hand front corner, tie with a slip knot
and fasten off with two or three half
hitches. This gives good tension along
the front edges.
27. Begin 18mm *(¾in)* from the front
left hand corner, pushing the needle
through on the line marked on the side
and coming out on the line marked on
the top. Bring the needle right out, then
push it back through as near to the left

hand corner as possible. Guide it so
that it comes out on the front line. Tie
an upholsterer's slip knot and pull the
twine up tightly.
28. For the next stitch, push in the
needle 2cm *(¾in)* to the right of the
first stitch. Guide the needle out on the
line drawn on the top.
29. Now pull the needle right through
and pass it back through the edge at
the place where the first stitch finished,
leaving it half-way through.

Wind the twine around the needle

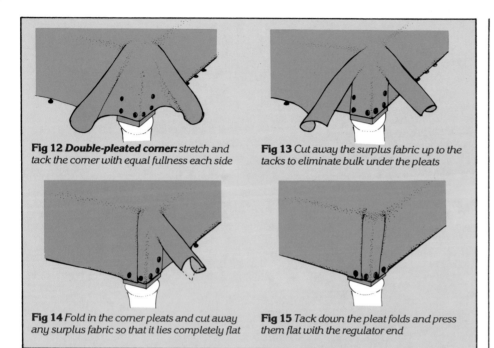

Fig 12 *Double-pleated corner:* *stretch and tack the corner with equal fullness each side*

Fig 13 *Cut away the surplus fabric up to the tacks to eliminate bulk under the pleats*

Fig 14 *Fold in the corner pleats and cut away any surplus fabric so that it lies completely flat*

Fig 15 *Tack down the pleat folds and press them flat with the regulator end*

three times and pull it up very tightly in the direction of the stitching (Fig 7a).
30. Continue across the front and up the right side, then work the left side and the back. Tie the twine end to those ends of twine left hanging on the 'blind' rows with a reef knot.

Fig 7b shows the shape you are working to achieve.

Top stuffing
31. Work stuffing ties across the seat as shown in Fig 8 and lightly pack stuffing under them. Notice that the stuffing 'feathers' off a little at the roll of the edge. It is very important that no hair is left hanging over the rolled edge.
32. To give support to the covering (and in particular the corner pleats), cut and fit some cardboard stiffeners. Use medium-thickness cardboard and cut two stiffeners to the shape shown in Fig 9. Tack the stiffeners round the corners.

Calico undercovering
33. The next step is the calico undercover, to pull down and contain the top stuffing, and to bring the seat to its finished shape. Fix the calico to the sides of the rails with no turnings.

Fold and tack the corners as shown in Fig 10.

Put one or two layers of cotton wadding on the undercovering to prevent the hair from coming through and to give a little more softness to the seat.

Top covering
34. Cut out a piece of fabric for the top cover and fold it in half twice. Clip the folded edges to mark the middle of all four sides. Spread the fabric right side up on the seat and fasten it temporarily with three or four tacks on each side.
35. Cut into the fabric at the back corners as shown in Fig 11 cutting to within 6mm *(¹⁄₄in)* of the wood. Take care when cutting surplus fabric: lay the fabric to see just how much can be cut away, then tuck and turn in the edges. Stretch down the turnings and temporarily tack them.

Double-pleated corners
36. Follow the diagrams in Fig 12 to Fig 15 for the method of working double-pleated front corners.

Stretch and tack the fabric at the corner as shown in Fig 12 so that there is an equal fullness at each side.
37. Cut away the surplus fabric up to the tacks to eliminate bulk under the pleats (Fig 13).
38. Fold in the pleats and, holding them down in turn with the regulator point, note where the fold comes at the bottom. Cut off any surplus fabric so that it lies as flat as possible (Fig 14).
39. Tack down the folds and then press them with the flat end of the regulator (Fig 15).

Finishing
Apply trimming to the chair.

Basic Skills 7

Hand-sewing stitches
A certain amount of hand-sewing is required in upholstery, particularly when a quality finish is required. However, it is only necessary to learn a few stitches and, if you can already sew a little, you will not find these at all difficult to master. This section also shows you how to cut fabric for making piped edges.

Lock stitch
This is a useful stitch and is used when it is necessary to seam areas of hessian together, such as where the arm and back of the chair meet, at the first stuffing stage.

The stitch consists of a series of small knots along the seam.

Use a fine No. 3 or No. 4 twine in a curved needle.
1. To start, make a straight stitch through both thicknesses of fabric. Taking the needle through both edges (Fig 1) and up through the loop of the twine, pull through to form the knot.
2. Make a straight stitch through both thicknesses, then make another knot.

Running stitch
Layers of hessian can also be attached to each other with simple running stitches. Fig 2 shows a long double-ended needle working the stitches. They should be of even length and with a space the length of a stitch between each of them.

Locking-back stitch
This is similar to blind edge stitch

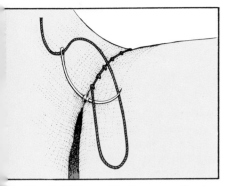

Fig 1 *Lock stitch* *consists of a series of knots worked along the seam using a curved needle*

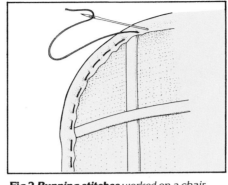

Fig 2 *Running stitches* *worked on a chair back. A double-ended needle is used*

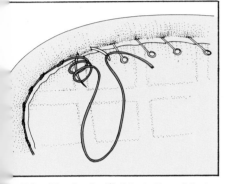

Fig 3 *Locking-back stitch* *is similar to blind edge stitches. Use it to join first stuffing to hessian*

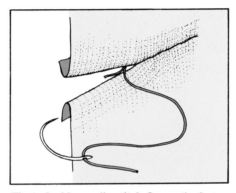

Fig 4a *Ladder or slip stitch:* *Secure the first small stitch with an upholsterer's slip knot*

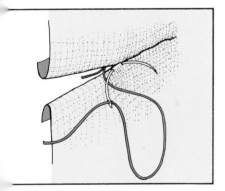

4b *Take a stitch through the fold of the over-lapping fabric back to the starting point*

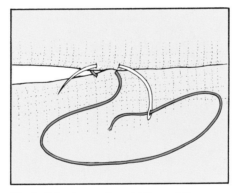

Fig 4c *Take the needle point through the opposite edge, a thread or two back from where the last stitch emerged*

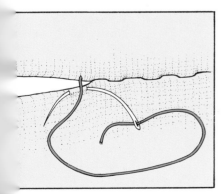

4d *Begin the next stitch a thread or two from where the needle last emerged. Pull thread tight after each stitch*

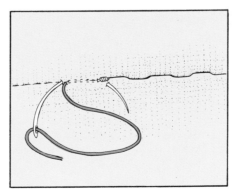

Fig 4e *Take two or three stitches back along the seam to finish. Cut thread end*

and is used when joining the first stuffing covering of scrim hessian to the basic support hessian, where stitched edges are to be formed (Fig 3 shows it on an armchair back).

Ladder or slip stitch

The length of a ladder stitch is determined by the fabric. For heavy, coarsely-woven fabrics, make stitches about 16mm (⅝in) long. When working on fine fabrics, a 5–10mm (³⁄₁₆–⅜in) stitch is neater.

A curved needle is used because the two fabric edges to be sewn are stretched taut and, usually, there is part of the wooden frame beneath.

1. Take a small stitch just beneath the overlapping covering fabric, 10mm (⅜in) to the right of the beginning of the seam. Secure the stitch with an upholsterer's slip knot (Fig 4a).
2. Take a stitch through the line of the fold of the overlapping fabric edge, back 10mm (⅜in). This secures the thread and hides the knot and the thread end, which are tucked away under the fold (Fig 4b).
3. Insert the needle point into the opposite folded edge, a thread or two back from the point where it last emerged (Fig 4c).
4. Continue making stitches in the same way, always inserting the needle a thread or two back, so that the thread disappears as it is pulled tightly after each stitch (Fig 4d).
5. Finishing: at the end of the seam, work a French knot, then take a few stitches back along the seam. Cut the thread end close to the fabric (Fig 4e).

Making piping

Piping is inserted into the edges of upholstered furniture and cushions to protect the fabric and provide an attractive finish. It is usual to make piping from the same fabric that has been used for the upholstery.

1. Spread the fabric and, using a long rule, mark the true bias of the fabric from the top right corner to the bottom left. Lay the ruler about 4cm (1½in) away and mark a parallel line. Continue marking strips on the fabric – they each should be at least 60cm (24in) long.
2. Cut out the strips, cutting the ends

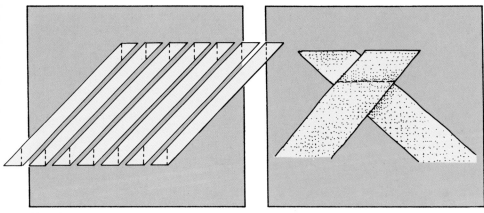

Fig 1 *Mark and cut the piping strips then cut ends as shown to reverse the angle*

Fig 2 *Machine the strips together as shown, right sides facing to make one long length*

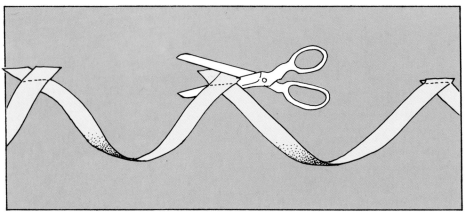

Fig 3 *Trim the seam allowances from the joins as shown*

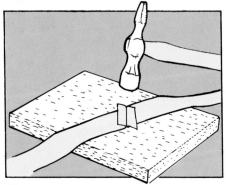

Fig 4 *Flatten the seam by tapping it with a hammer on a hardwood block*

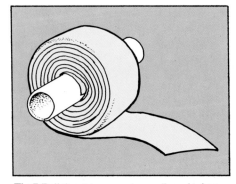

Fig 5 *Roll the strip around a cardboard tube to keep it manageable and clean*

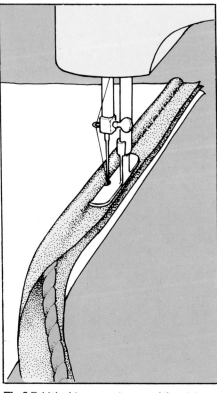

Fig 6 *Fold the bias-cut strips round the piping cord then machine-stitch*

to reverse the angle. This can be seen in Fig 1, marked with a broken line.

3. When you have cut the required number of strips, machine-stitch them together, right sides facing, to make one long length (Fig 2). Trim the seam allowance (Fig 3). Press the seams open, or tap the seams with a broad-faced hammer, working on a hardwood block (Fig 4).

4. Roll the strip of piping fabric round a cardboard tube to keep it tidy (Fig 5).

5. With the piping foot on the machine, stitch the folded fabric round the piping (Fig 6).

Note: For size 1 (stout) piping cord, piping strips need to be 37mm (*1½in*) wide. Thicker to thinner cords correspondingly need wider or narrower strips to be cut, to provide the seam allowance required on the finished piping.

Incorporating piping into a seam

The diagram (Fig 7) shows piping being fitted into an arm front scroll facing but the method is the same for other piping seams.

1. Fix the piping with pins beneath the lip of the scroll's edge. Cut the facing fabric to shape and fix it in the position, folding in the edge, and using the same pins, removing each in turn, but catching in the folded-in edge of the facing. Sew in the facing, using a curved needle and ladder stitch. Take stitches through the seam allowance of the piping (along the line of machine stitches), each time a stitch is made in the facing or the inside off the scroll lip (Fig 7).

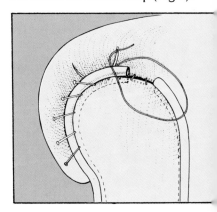

Fig 7 *Fix piping in place with pins, sew in the facing cover and piping together using ladder stitches*

Fabric-covered piping edges the settee and its back and seat cushions

Basic Skills 8

Needlework covers

If you enjoy needlework you may perhaps consider embroidering covers for a set of dining room chairs or for an occasional chair and this can be a rewarding upholstery project. Having chosen a suitable design, prepare the canvas so that the embroidery is worked to the shape required.

Basic technique

Making the template

Cut a piece of brown paper to roughly the size and shape of the chair seat, including the seat sides. Crease the paper both horizontally and vertically. Skewer the paper to the seat, keeping the creases centred. Draw the outline of the seat onto the paper and cut it to fit around the chair back uprights (and chair front uprights if the chair has these). Fold the paper down over the seat sides and mark the line where the upholstery meets the show wood. To shape the paper to the seat, pleat the edges and pin (see Fig 1).

Remove the paper from the chair (retaining the pinned pleats) and trim. Spread on a fresh sheet of paper. Trace round the outline and cut it out. Now, fold the new pattern vertically and horizontally to mark the centre (Fig 2).

Preparing for embroidery

Measure and mark the centre of the canvas with vertical and horizontal lines of basting threads.

Position the cut-out template on the canvas and mark the outline with a waterproof pen. Keep the template, because you will be using it again at a later stage.

Work the embroidery two or three rows of stitches outside the marked outline.

Preparing for upholstery

Complete the upholstery of the chair to the point where the top fabric is to be put on.

Trace the paper template onto tracing paper, marking in the vertical and horizontal crease lines. Now try the tracing over the finished embroidery to see if there has been any distortion during working. If distortion has occurred, the embroidered canvas will have to be re-shaped and blocked before it can be used on the chair.

Blocking canvas

If the needlework is very distorted, it must be stretched and pressed. You will need a piece of plywood which is a little larger than the canvas. Cover this with two layers of white blotting paper and pencil in a rectangle (or square) the exact size of the canvas on the top layer. Lay the needlework face-down on the paper-covered board. Using 13mm (1/2in) improved tacks, tack the front edge along the front edge line on the paper. Set tacks 4cm (1 1/2in) apart. The tacks should be set only halfway home. Tack the right-hand edge of the embroidered canvas. By gently stretching the canvas out, you will be able to tack the left-hand edge and then the back edge (Fig 3).

When the needlework is tacked square, dampen a pressing cloth and spread it over the work. Using a very hot iron, press until the cloth is dry. After pressing, leave the needlework on the board to dry naturally, then remove the tacks and proceed with top covering the upholstery.

Note: If you have difficulty in stretching exactly to the pencilled lines, stretch and tack as far as possible, then press and, while the work is still hot and damp, remove the back edge and side edge lines of tacks and stretch the canvas up to the pencilled lines, then re-tack.

Drop-in chair seats

Embroidered canvas can be used for covering this type of chair seat but, as the fabric is likely to be thicker than the used previously, it may be necessary to plane some of the wood away to ensure a good fit when the seat is placed into the frame.

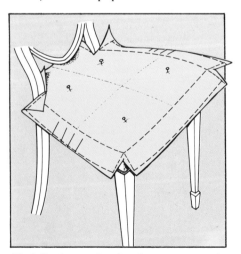

Fig 1 *Cut the template from brown paper, and cut and pleat it to fit the seat shape*

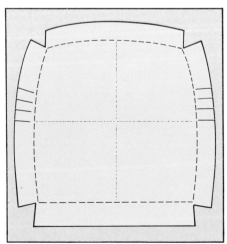

Fig 2 *The template should look something like this when removed from the seat*

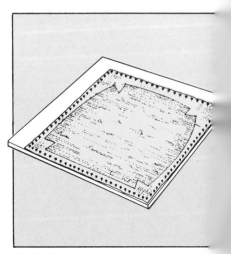

Fig 3 *If blocking is necessary, tack the canvas to a board, stretching it into shape*

Late Regency carver chair upholstered in Bargello embroidery, a pattern called 'Carnation'

Fireside Stool

This project repeats many of the methods used for the stuffed-over seat chair and will help you to practise the fastening of webbing and hessian, building up horsehair edges and stitching a roll edge. Then there are variations of the techniques to stretch your upholstery skills just a little bit more.

Preparation

1. Remove the old upholstery and tacks.
2. Fasten the new webbing and tarpaulin hessian.
3. Put in the stuffing ties and build the wall of horsehair so that it overhangs the frame by about 18mm *(¾in)*. Extending the width and length of the seat by this amount gives a better balance between the upholstery and the curved legs (see the picture).
4. Cover the first stuffing with scrim. Regulate the stuffing.
5. Work the through stuffing ties.

Edge-stitching

6. Work the corners of the stool so that they are more rounded (see the picture). Work three rows of 'blind' stitches all round the stool (Fig 1).
7. Work a roll edge.

Top stuffing

8. Work stuffing ties across the stool, down its length. The top stuffing should be long stranded horsehair arranged to a depth of at least 7.5cm *(3in)*.

Undercover

9. The calico undercover is not tacked down onto the frame but temporarily fastened with skewers, and is then sewn down with locking-back stitches under the lip of the roll edge. The reason for doing this is because the stool is to have a 'convexed' border which will be recessed under the roll edge.

Top cover

10. Overlay the calico with two layers of cotton wadding. The top cover is then fastened over this.
11. Work a row of gently-tensioned stuffing ties along the stool border, midway between the show wood of the frame and the roll edge. Work horsehair under the ties thinly and evenly, to round out the border.
12. Cut strips of wadding long enough to go all round the border and deep enough to have a turning on the top and bottom edges, to fit under the roll and cover the border stuffing. Fig 2 shows the various stages of working the border and a detail of this.

Covering the border

13. Cut a strip of covering fabric to fit round the stool, joining two strips if necessary. Pin it over the stuffing.

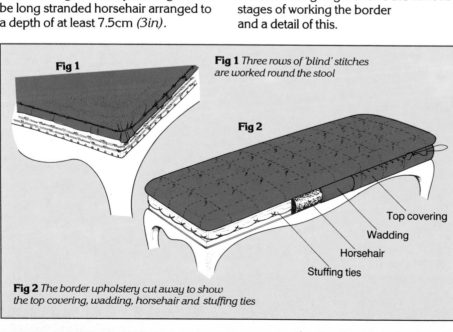

Fig 1 *Three rows of 'blind' stitches are worked round the stool*

Fig 2

Top covering
Wadding
Horsehair
Stuffing ties

Fig 2 *The border upholstery cut away to show the top covering, wadding, horsehair and stuffing ties*

Temporary tack, then sew the covering under the roll edge using ladder stitches with thread in a 7.5cm *(3in)* 17 gauge curved needle. When working the stitches, take the needle into the seat edge, pushing it in deeply so that the thread catches the scrim hessian forming the stitched edge. If this is done, the top edge of the border fabric will be recessed and pulled well in. At a point about 7.5cm *(3in)* from one corner, make an extra long ladder stitch about 13mm *(½in)* long). (This is where the end of the decorative trimming cord can be tucked away.) Mark the place with a pin. Finish the border by permanently tacking down the bottom edge.

Trimming

14. Decorative chair cord has been used to trim the stool pictured. Begin by inserting one end through the marked Ladder stitch on the seam. Pin in place, then stretch the cord tightly round the stool. Secure with a pin about 5cm *(2in)* from the beginning. Allow sufficient cord to be inserted into the same gap, then wind self-adhesive tape around the cord and cut through it. Tuck the cord end into the gap. Pin the cord at 7.5cm *(3in)* intervals into the stool and then sew it in place, finishing off with a French knot.

Apply a good quality braid to cover the tacks that finish the bottom edge of the border. Sew the braid in place.

Tools and materials required for this project

Tools: Ripping chisel and mallet, sharp knife and scissors, webbing stretcher, heavy and light hammers, 10cm *(4in)* curved needle, 25cm *(10in)* double-pointed needle and 7.5cm *(3in)* 19 gauge cording needle, 7.5cm *(3in)* 17 gauge curved needle, regulator, upholstery gauge, felt-tipped marker.
Materials: webbing, hessian, horsehair, scrim, calico, wadding, top covering, trimming and adhesive, 16mm *(⅝in)* and 13mm *(½in)* improved tacks, 10mm *(⅜in)* fine tacks, No. 1 and No. 3 twine.

Basic skills used in this project

Ripping off – page 16
Webbing – page 18
Fastening hessian – page 20
Stuffing ties – page 20
Stuffing – page 21
Edge-stitching and roll edges – page 37
Building up stuffing – page 21
Putting on wadding – page 44
Applying undercovering – page 21
Applying top covering – page 23
Applying trimming – page 24

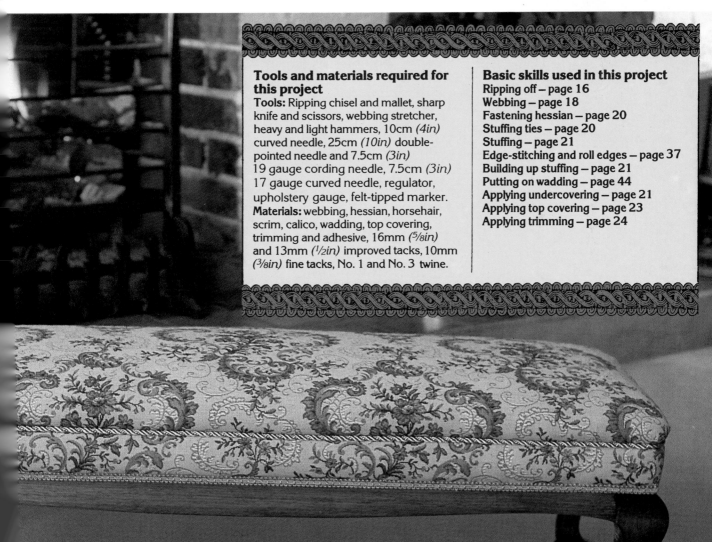

Basic Skills 9

Making cushions

Soft luxurious scatter cushions make upholstered furniture even more comfortable and, at the same time, provide colour and pattern accents to a furnishing scheme. In this section, you are shown how to make simple scatter cushions and well-fitting box cushions for chairs, window seats and sofas.

Scatter cushions

Square or rectangular scatter cushions can be very simply made.

Cut two pieces of fabric the same size and shape. Pin and machine-stitch them together, right sides facing, starting about 5cm (2in) from one corner. Work round three sides, finishing 5cm (2in) from the corner on the fourth side.

Neaten the seam allowances and cut off the corners diagonally. Turn the cushion cover to the right side, insert the cushion pad and close the open seam with slip stitches.

Fastenings

If a more professional finish is required, a zip fastener or press fastening tape can be inserted into a seam. This is easiest to do before the cushion is made up.

Stitch the zip fastener between the two cushion cover pieces (or stitch the tape along the edges on the right side) (Fig 1). Then make up the cushion cover as described.

Round or oval cushions

These can also be made using the basic method described for square or rectangular cushions. Zip fasteners are best inserted into the back of the cushion.

Cut the front piece to size, then cut the back piece in two halves with an extra 13mm (½in) on each of the straight edges. Insert the zip fastener between the edges so that the back becomes the same size as the front.

Make up the cushion cover as described.

Tucked opening

This method can be used for cushions of any shape. Cut the front piece to size, then cut the back piece in two sections. Cut one an extra 2.5cm (1in) on the inside edge and the other with an extra 5cm (2in) on the inside edge. Turn a neat machine-stitched hem on both edges.

Place the sections together, overlapping, so that the back is the same size as the front. Machine-stitch together at the top and bottom edges (Fig 2). Make up the cushion in the way described, then turn to the right side

through the open back flap. The opening can be fastened with a button and loop, or ribbon ties if desired.

Fitted box cushions

These can be made to fit an armchair or a settee, or for a window seat. A perfect fit is the aim and this is achieved by first preparing a paper template.

Making the template

Use strong paper – brown wrapping paper is ideal – and measuring the seat, cut a piece of paper to roughly the right dimensions. Fold the paper in half, then half again, pressing in the creases. Open out the paper again.

Spread the paper on the chair and carefully draw the outline of the seat on the paper. If the front (or back) uprights cut into the seat, press the paper round the upright and then mark it with the

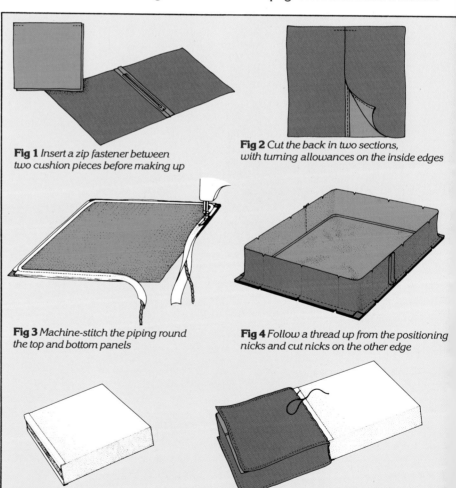

Fig 1 *Insert a zip fastener between two cushion pieces before making up*

Fig 2 *Cut the back in two sections, with turning allowances on the inside edges*

Fig 3 *Machine-stitch the piping round the top and bottom panels*

Fig 4 *Follow a thread up from the positioning nicks and cut nicks on the other edge*

Fig 5 *Glue calico strips along the front edges of the rubber foam pad*

Fig 6 *Attach the interior pad to the front border of the cushion cover*

...ped piped box cushions make comfortable ...ing on a window seat

...ncil. Cut out on the pencilled line so ...t the template exactly fits the seat ...d fits round the uprights.

...Fold the paper vertically to see if the ...t and left sides match. You may ...d to do some trimming.

...For a sofa or window seat cushions, ... a single template of the entire seat. ...s can be cut into the number of cushions required. The two end templates are then laid together and their sizes compared for trimming. Only one template need be used for shaping both cushions. The template (or templates) you have made should be the exact size of the finished cushion, including piped edges.

Cutting out

Lay the template on the fabric, making sure that the creases in the paper follow the straight grain of the fabric. Mark round the shape with tailor's chalk. Cut out exactly 10mm *(3/8in)* away from the chalked line. Use this cut-out piece of fabric to cut out the other side of the cushion and keep the template as you will need it for cutting out the foam interior.

Place both panels together, right sides facing and cut positioning V's, three on each edge. This will enable you to position the border accurately.

Piping

Measure round the cushion panels and estimate the amount of piping you will need. Prepare the piping (see page 40).

Applying piping

Start applying the piping somewhere on the right-hand edge to ensure that there is no join showing on the front face.

Pin, and machine-stitch the piping along the chalked seam line. As the corners are reached, lay the piping along the fabric and make a small nick in the piping's seam allowance (Fig 3 page 46). This enables the piping to turn the corner neatly, ready to be worked along the next edge.

Machine-stitch the piping from the starting point (Fig 3) but stop and remove the work from the machine about 10cm *(4in)* from the end. Lay the work flat, then trim the piping cord so that the ends butt. Cut back the piping strip ends so that they overlap about 2cm *(¾in)*. (The line of the cut should be the same as that of the joins in the strip.) Now machine-stitch the cut ends together.

Refold the fabric over the piping cord and complete the stitching. Pipe round both cushion panels in the same way.

Cushion borders

Assuming that the box cushion is to have an interior pad 10cm *(4in)* deep, the finished depth of the cushion will be 9cm *(3½in)*. This will give tension to the cushion face. Cut the fabric for the borders 10.1cm *(4¼in)* deep. Measure the four sides of the cushion and add 2.5 cm *(1in)* to the measurement. Cut the fabric. Join the short ends. The join should be on the side of the cushion (see Fig 4).

Start pinning the panel to the border piece, right sides facing, starting at centre front. When the corner is reached, clip into the border edge so that a neat corner can be made (see Fig 4). Machine-stitch the border to the panel, panel side uppermost, using the piping foot and keeping the stitches just inside those made to hold the piping. Cut V's on the other edge of the border to correspond with the V's on the top panel.

Attach the bottom panel in the same way, matching V's but leaving the entire back edge and about 9cm *(3½in)* at each adjoining side unstitched, so that the interior pad can be inserted.

Neaten the seam allowances.

Now work an extra line of machine-stitches along the piping at the cover mouth to tighten the piping.

Preparing the interior pad

Rubber foam block is recommended for cushion interior pads – it lasts longer than plastic foam and is more resilient. Use the brown paper template to cut the block to shape. Lay the template on the foam and mark round it, 10mm *(⅜in)* away using a felt-tipped pen. Cut out the shape using a fine-toothed panel saw.

Fastening the cover

Tear two strips of calico 6cm *(2½in)*

wide and long enough to go across the front of the interior pad. Coat the strips with soft bond adhesive and also coat the top and bottom edges of the interior pad (see Fig 5). Leave for a few minutes until the adhesive is dry to the touch, then lay the strips over the edges and press in place.

Now position the interior pad and cushion cover together as shown in Fig 6. Note that the seam allowances are turned in so that they lie against the border. Temporarily fix the cover and pad together with skewers, then sew them together with large stitches. The stitches go through the calico strips, about 3mm *(1/8in)* from the edge and the same distance from the cushion cover piping stitches. Adjust the seam allowances so that they lie on the borders to help the piping to stand well.

Pull the cushion cover over the interior pad, adjusting the fit with your hand as you work. Close the opening with small ladder stitches.

Soft square cushions massed on a deep window seat in plain and patterned fabric.

Prie Dieu Chair

Prie Dieu or prayer chairs were designed for kneeling on and the upholstered platform tops served as arm, or prayer book, rests. This project demonstrates how a spring seat is worked and how bordering is done. Other techniques used have already been covered in previous chapters.

Preparation

1. Having stripped the frame, web the chair seat and back (Fig 1).
2. Fasten tarpaulin hessian on the back then fasten the stuffing ties on the back about 2.5cm *(1in)* from the frame edges (Fig 2).
3. Look at the picture of the chair and then begin to build a consolidated wall of horsehair to the shape and depth of the edge as it will be when the upholstery is finished. The hair should overhang the frame by about 6mm *(1/4in)* see Fig. 3.

4. Fill up the centre part of the back and the top shelf to the depth of the edges.
5. Cover the first stuffing with scrim hessian and then put in the 'through stuffing' ties as shown in Fig 4.

For the scale of the chair pictured, the thickness of the edges is 4cm *(1 1/2in)* from the tacking chamfer giving a total depth, including the wood of the frame, of 6cm *(2 1/2in)*.

Stitching the edges

6. Put in two rows of 'blind stitches' and one row of through stitches, to form the roll. Precision is important in this chair

so straight even rows of stitches must be made, following the lines of the threads in the scrim wherever possible.

Springs

7. The chair pictured has eight, 15cm *(6in)* 12 gauge springs (see Fig 6, page 53. When building springs into a chair seat, bear in mind the build (particularly the weight) of the user and if necessary use stouter gauge springs. Nine is the usual number of springs for a rectangular seat but the shape of the Prie Dieu's seat makes one less spring necessary. Fasten the springs to the webbing and lace them down.

Covering the springs

8. The strongest tarpaulin hessian is used for the spring cover. Measure and cut the hessian allowing 3cm *(1 1/4in)* all round for turnings. Using 13mm *(1/2in)* improved tacks, temporary tack three tacks at the centre of the back rail three at the front rail and three at the centre of each of the side rails, setting tacks about 4cm *(1 1/2in)* apart. Pull at the corners with a gentle tension and temporarily fasten, making an oblique cut into the corners of both back uprights.
9. Now begin to drive in the permanent tacks along the back rail at intervals of about 5cm *(2in)*. Complete the permanent tacking on the front and side rails, keeping a gentle tension. Tension the corners, removing the temporary tacks there and then tack permanently. Turn in the edges and tack down through the double thickness of hessian with the tacks positioned between those already put.

Fasten the springs with stout twine (No. 1), through the hessian with three knotted stitches per spring. Put in the stuffing ties for the edge hair (Fig 7).
10. Work horsehair under the ties very firmly and evenly, slightly overhanging

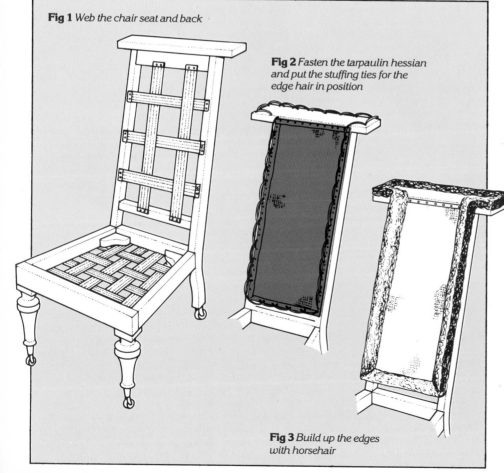

Fig 1 *Web the chair seat and back*

Fig 2 *Fasten the tarpaulin hessian and put the stuffing ties for the edge hair in position*

Fig 3 *Build up the edges with horsehair*

ols: ripping chisel and mallet, sharp
ife and scissors, side-cutting pliers,
k hammer and heavier hammer,
ebbing stretcher, spring needle,
gulator, upholstery gauge, skewers and
ns, 25cm *(10in)* double-pointed needle,
cm *(4in)* curved needle, 7.5cm *(3in)*
gauge curved needle, 7.5cm *(3in)*
gauge curved needle. **Materials:**
ebbing, 15cm *(6in)* 12 gauge springs,
paulin hessian, scrim, No. 1 and No. 3
ine, laid cord, horsehair, wadding,
ssian, black bottom lining, unbleached
lico, top covering fabric, trimming and
hesive, sewing thread or yarn.

asic skills used in this project

*Prie Dieu, late nineteenth century, upholstered
in striped damask*

the frame size. Then fill the centre of the seat, doming it slightly.

Scrim cover

11. Put on the scrim cover, measuring and checking the height of the edges of the seat as you tack. Tacking accurately to the weave of the scrim at the front and the back and work the sides from the front corners towards the back. The through stuffing ties are put through to the spring hessian only (Fig 8).

Edge-stitching the seat

12. Two rows of blind stitching and two 'through' rows are worked to give the edge the extra firmness required. After working the two blind rows regulate the filling then mark a line 4cm (1½in) in from the edge. Start with a single stitch on the right hand corner (refer to the Stuffed-over seat on page 34 for the technique). Stitch the front edge first, with stitches 22mm (⅞in) in length and close together. Continue along the right hand side to the back, then down the left hand edge. When this first 'through' row is complete use the regulator to bring the edge up again and then mark another line 2cm (¾in) in from the edge to guide your second row of 'through' stitches which will be 15mm (⅝in) in length and adjoining each other following the same sequence as with the first row.

Top stuffing

13. Four rows of looped stuffing ties are worked. Long, stranded, curly horsehair should be used for the top stuffing. Tease it well, then work it under the

Detail of inside corner of top platform showing complete roll edge and gusset set into the hessian at the inside corner

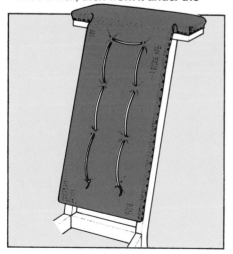

Fig 4 *Cover the whole of the back with scrim hessian and put in the 'through' stuffing ties*

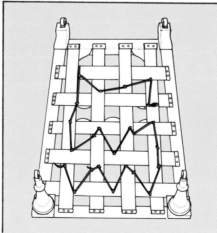

Fig 5 *Fasten the springs from under the webbing with No. 1 stout twine*

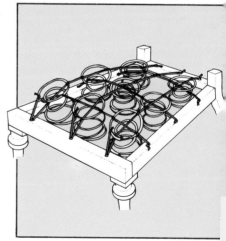

Fig 6 *The position of the seat springs when laced, and the method of lacing with laid cord*

This detail shows the sharpness of the corner and the well-defined roll edge

seat's stuffing ties (Fig 9). Don't use too much hair because the finished upholstery should be fairly flat.

Calico undercover

14. Cut the calico to size and tightly stretch it over the stuffing, temporarily tacking it along the back rail and skewering it under the roll edge lip at the sides and front. Adjust the tension and sew the undercover beneath the roll edge all round using a locking backstitch with a 10cm *(4in)* curved needle and fine twine. Permanently tack the calico along the back rail. Work the back of the chair in the same way.

Top covering

15. Spread 2 layers of cotton wadding over the back and over the seat. Measure and cut the top covering fabric (marking it for centring). Spread the fabric and sew in place, as you did for the undercover, tensioning it slightly.
16. When cutting into the two inside corners of the top shelf and the two back corners of the seat at the back upright, extra care should be taken. Cut just far enough to allow the fabric to 'lay in'. Remember to tension the fabric diagonally, pulling gently at the corners, for tight, even edges.

Bordering

In this chair, the borders are sewn almost on the extreme edge of the seat and on the back upholstery, producing a squared 'boxed' look.

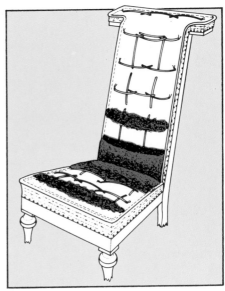

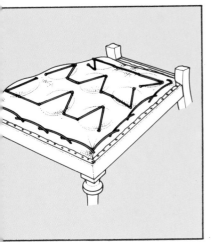

7 *Tarpaulin hessian is stretched over the ings. Fasten them with No. 1 stout twine and in the stuffing ties for the edge hair*

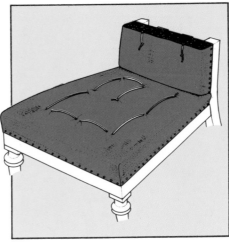

Fig 8 *Stuff the seat with horsehair and cover it with scrim hessian. Put the 'through' stuffing ties in position*

Fig 9 *Flat layer of top stuffing worked under stuffing ties of seat and back*

Stuffing the borders

17. Tear cotton wadding lengthways so that a folded strip can be used around the complete length of the border, avoiding lumpy joins. Apply three layers of the wadding on each border. Stretch each piece of wadding and secure at the end with pins, (which you must remember to take out when covering.)

Covering borders

18. Cut the fabric to cover the platform shelf border plus 13mm (1/2in) allowance on the long sides. Turn in the edge and stretch tightly round, fastening with upholsterer's pins, and with tacks at the two inside corners.

19. Pin the top edge of the border all the way along in a straight line at the very edge of the back covering. Tack the bottom edge with 10m (3/8in) fine tacks, tacking well under the platform. Ladder-stitch the top seam of this border with small stitches.

20. Cut, fit and pin the two pieces to form the side borders of the back. Tack the bottom edges to the frame. After tacking the back edges behind the back uprights, the pinned seams can be sewn.

21. Sew up the joins at the two top inside corners (where the sides meet the top border) with very small Ladder stitches as these seams will have no trimming to hide them.

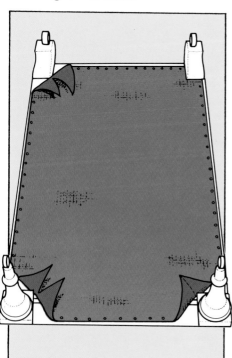

Fig 10 *Cut the bottom cover neatly at the corners*

Cording: the decorative chair cord on the seat border is tucked away into the join between the seat and the back before the back border cord is applied

Lastly, work the seat border. (If the
t is too wide for the fabric, join
es so that the seams are at the front
ners where they will be less
spicuous.)

Stretch the border fabric round the
t very tightly and tack the two ends
ind the back uprights. Fold in the
edge and pin, right up to the angle
he edge.

The bottom edge has to be tacked
eath the seat so cut carefully to
w for folding in at the front and back
s. (Make the cuts at an angle
quely, starting from near the middle
he legs.) Ladder-stitch this border.

tside back panels

Cut a small piece of fabric to cover
underside of the back platform
lf. (Turn the chair upside-down to
ition this piece. Turn in the edges
d pin along the back and side edges
he shelf.) You can tack where the
ck meets the underside of the shelf.
lder-stitch the pinned edges.

Tack a piece of 275g *(10oz)*
sian tightly over the outside back
ne (this will form a reinforcement for
back panel covering). Over this
ead one thickness of cotton
dding.

Measure and cut the covering fabric
owing 2.5cm *(1in)* all round for
nings. Turn in the top edge and pin
he chair. Tension the fabric
wnwards and temporarily tack
eath the bottom rail.

Cut into the fabric to fit around the
ck legs and then turn in the sides,
ning it on right up to the edges. At
bottom corners, fasten the fabric
h gimp pins driven part way in,
und which you can wind the yarn at
end of the rows of Ladder stitches.
en drive the gimp pins home.

Ladder-stitch the back panel in
ce then drive home the temporary
ks beneath the bottom rail.

e bottom cover

Use a good quality lining cloth, such
medium-weight black platform
tton fabric.

Use 10mm *(3/8in)* fine tacks and tack
bottom cover in place, cutting the
ric neatly at the corners (see Fig 10).

Trim the chair seat and back edges
h cord, positioning it right on the
reme edges. Fasten a matching
id around the bottom edge of the seat.

Buttoned-seat Stool

A simple, rectangular dressing table stool is used for this project, as
an introduction to the art of buttoned upholstery. The dimensions of
the stool top pictured are unlikely to be exactly the same as your
own stool and the number of buttons and their arrangement may
therefore need to be adjusted accordingly.

Preparation

1. Remove the old upholstery and tacks.
2. Fasten the new webbing and
tarpaulin hessian in place.
(The stool pictured on page 57 has four
pieces of webbing one way and three
interwoven the other),

Recessed first stuffing

3. The first stuffing is recessed into the
stool to give depth to the buttoning. To
prepare for this, mark a line on the
tarpaulin hessian 7.5cm *(3in)* in from
the edges all round. To determine the
amount of scrim required, measure the
marked rectangle and add 17cm *(7in)*
all round. Cut a piece of scrim to exactly
this size.
4. Draw a rectangle on the scrim the
same size as that marked on the
hessian, and centred exactly.

5. Next, draw a line 2.5cm *(1in)* in from
the edges of the scrim. This is the
tacking line. Try to make sure that the
marked lines on the scrim follow the
straight grain of the fabric.
6. Spread the scrim on the tarpaulin
hessian and sew the two fabrics
together, line to line, with long running
stitches, working them about 13mm
(1/2in) long (Fig 1).
7. Now fold the scrim onto the seat (see
Fig 2) and secure with skewers.

Stuffing ties

8. Work stuffing ties around the stool
about 2.5cm *(1in)* in from the edge.
Pack horsehair under the ties to make a
wall all round.
9. Now release the scrim from the
skewers in the centre of the seat and
spread it over the wall of hair (Fig 3).
Fasten the scrim temporarily with tacks.

Tools and materials required for this project

Tools: ripping chisel and mallet, sharp
knife, pointed scissors, lightweight hammer,
heavier hammer, 10cm *(4in)*, curved
needle, 7.5cm *(3in)* curved cording
needle, 25cm *(10in)* double-pointed
needle, regulator, upholstery gauge and
felt-tipped marker, chalk, 2 button fold
sticks, steel tape rule, skewers, long rule.
Materials: tarpaulin hessian, webbing,
scrim, horsehair, cotton wadding,
polyester wadding, buttons, top fabric,
braid trim, nylon twine.

Basic skills used in this project

Ripping off – page 16
Webbing – page 18
Fastening tarpaulin hessian – page 20
Specially recessed first stuffing –
page 55
Stuffing ties – page 21
Stuffing – page 21
Applying top covering – page 23
Simple buttonwork – page 58

Fold the fabric under on the tacking line and permanently tack with 10mm (³⁄₈in) fine tacks. Tack the fabric true to the chamfer on the frame's edge.

10. Fold the corners as shown in Fig 3.

11. Work edge-stitching all round the stool, working two 'blind' rows of stitches. Work a third row of stitches for the roll edge.

Top stuffing

12. Put in the stuffing ties for the top stuffing (see Fig 4). Pack good quality curled horsehair under the ties firmly. The domed centre should be at least 4cm (1¹⁄₂in) above the level of the edges. Take care to fill right up to the edges so that, when compressed by gentle pressure of the hand, no hollowness can be felt near the edges.

Make sure that no hair extends over the roll edge.

13. Overlay the horsehair with a layer of cotton wadding, trimming it so that it wraps over the roll edge and hangs level with the line of tacks on the tacking chamfer.

14. Over this, spread a piece of polyester wadding, stretching it with a little tension and fastening the edges near to the bottom of the seat rails with tacks.

Planning the button positions

15. Eleven buttons were used for the stool pictured but it is unlikely that you will be able to apply these instructions exactly to your own stool. When setting out, the number of buttons and their positions will be different.

Measure and mark the exact centre of the stool top. Push in a skewer at this point. From the centre, the other button positions can be planned.

To decide a pleasing arrangement that will suit the shape and size of your stool top, place skewers in a rough diamond pattern, just to see the effect. Change their positioning until you feel that you have settled on the best arrangement. Now, measure and mark the positions with tailor's chalk. As a guide, the distance from the buttons to the edges should be no more than the width between the buttons and no less than half this measurement (Fig 5).

16. Using pointed scissors, make holes in the marked places, big enough to get at least two fingers in, and right throug to the hessian beneath.

Setting out the underside

17. Turn the stool over and mark the button positions on the webbing and hessian, using a felt-tipped pen (Fig 6

18. Following Fig 7 and, adapting the measurement to your own stool, mak a similar plan on paper, noting all the measurements you need – the distanc between buttons and their distance from the edges. From the plan, you wi be able to work out how much fabric you require for the top covering.

Measuring

19. Take a flexible steel tape rule, and place the end of it into a button hole nearest to one side of the stool. Holdin the measure so that it is touching the platform hessian, bend it over the edg and take it 2.5cm (1in) under the seat rail. Take this measurement and enter on your plan (A). Repeat this procedu measuring to the front (B) and to the back (C) and enter the measurements

On the covering material, a greater distance must be allowed between the

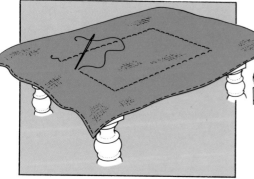

Fig 1 Sew the two fabrics together with long running stitches, working them about 13mm (¹⁄₂in) long

Fig 2 Fold the scrim into the centre of the seat. Make a horsehair wall all round, under the ties

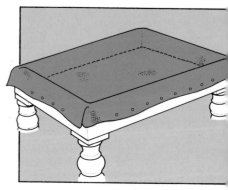

Fig 3 Release the scrim from the centre, spread over the hair and fasten with temporary tacks

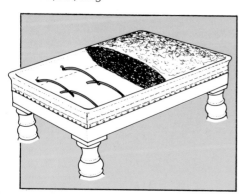

Fig 4 Work two rows of 'blind' stitches and one roll edge row. Put in stuffing ties for top stuffing

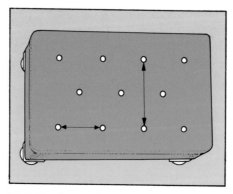

Fig 5 The distance from the buttons to edges should be no more than width between them and no less than half that measurement

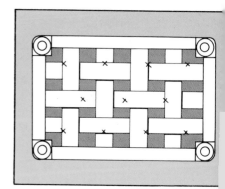

Fig 6 Mark the button positions on the webbing and hessian as shown here. Use a felt-tipped pen

...uttoned dressing table stool in English cherry ...ood, covered in tapestry

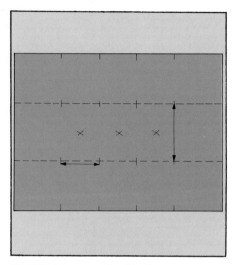

Fig 7 *Make a paper plan like this, noting down all the measurements you need*

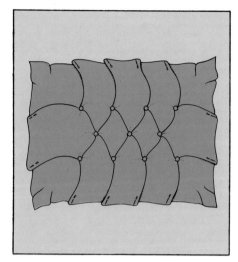

Fig 8 *All the folds between the buttons are made to face outwards from the centre*

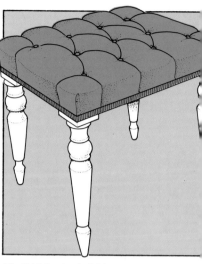

Fig 9 *Make single fold pleats at the corners the stool. Finish with a trim of braid*

marks for the buttons than the distance between the button holes in the upholstery. The difference is what is called the 'between button allowance'. This extra length and width to the diamond shape allows the fabric and the buttons to sink into the button holes. The 'between button allowance' can vary from 2.5cm *(1in)* to 5cm *(2in)*, depending on how deep the work is required to be.

In Fig 7, an allowance of 32mm *(1¼in)* has been made in the length and width of each diamond shape.
20. From the completed plan, add the measurements and work out the size of the fabric required for the top covering.
21. Spread the fabric right-side down and, using a long ruler and tailor's chalk, set out the cover exactly as your plan. Check your measurements at least twice to make sure they are correct. Then, using a regulator, make holes in the fabric at the button marks, so that the holes can be clearly seen on the right side. Note the edge marks on

the plan in Fig 7. Make similar marks on your fabric.
22. Have the buttons made up from offcuts of the cover fabric.

Putting in the buttons
23. Thread the 25cm *(10in)*-long double-pointed needle with a long length of nylon twine. Begin with the centre button. From the underside of the stool, insert the needle a little to off-centre of the mark and bring the needle to the top side through the centre hole of the cover. Thread on a button and reinsert the needle in the same hole, through the cover and the stuffing, so that it emerges on the other side of the centre mark on the underside.
24. Hold both of the twine ends that are now protruding through underneath with one hand and, with the other, hold the button away from the surface of the cover to make sure that there are no twists in the twine. Still holding the button so that it cannot twist round, draw it into the hole, taking the covering

fabric down, but not too deeply.

The twine is now clear of the wadd so that it cannot bind itself to the wadding when this is pulled through

From the underside, draw one en the twine through until you have a length of about 15cm *(6in)*, then tie upholsterer's slip knot. Cut and roll u piece of webbing to make a 'toggle' place this behind the slip knot to prevent the twine from cutting the webbing and hessian. Draw the butt in a little more but do not lock the sli knot, just cut off the twine end so tha the draw cord is longer (and you will know which one to pull later).

Follow this procedure with the remaining two buttons of the central row, then complete a side row.

Making button folds
To make the diagonal folds between the buttons, you will need two regulators (or two flat wooden butto fold sticks). Note that in Fig 8, all the folds between the buttons are facing outwards from the centre.
25. Hold one flat end of a regulator under the fabric and tuck the other regulator into the fold. By working th fabric in from button to button, neat folds can be made and any bunchin the fabric smoothed out.
26. Next, put in the other row of buttons, using the regulator again to in the folds neatly and with the openings in the correct directions. (Note that you can only use one regulator for this stage because you cannot now get under the cover.)
27. Give each of the button draw cor

a tug at this juncture to make all the buttons lie at the same depth.

28. At each of the edge marks, make a fold as shown in Fig 8.

As the 'between button allowance' on the stool pictured is 32mm *(1¼in)*, folds will have to be made of 16mm *(⁵⁄₈in)*. Pin these folds near to the edges.

29. Taking each fold in turn, pull them down and under, at the same time using the end of the regulator to ease the folds in.

Several attempts may have to be made before the folds lie evenly and the wrinkles have been smoothed out. Temporary tack each fold under the seat.

30. As the corners are square, a single fold pleat looks neat (Fig 9).

Single fold pleat

Follow the diagrams (Fig 10) to make a single fold pleat.

Put one temporary tack to the side of the corner (a). Cut the fabric at the angle shown so that it can be taken under the seat rail and neatly folded at the side rail and front leg junction. Temporary tack and cut off surplus fabric (b).

Fold the fabric under and bring it round the leg corner, fastening with two tacks on the leg top front. Place the tacks at least 2cm *(¾in)* in from the corner (c). Cut off the surplus fabric (d).

Fold in the pleat so that its edge is on the corner. Hold down with the regulator and cut off the surplus fabric from the doubled thickness at the bottom of the pleat. Cut also up to the front rail and leg junction (e).

Fasten the pleat with two tacks. Sew up the pleats with small ladder stitches

. Pull all the buttons down tightly and fasten off each slip knot with three half stitches.

. Trim off the surplus twine (but not so much that the knots will come undone). Tighten and permanently tack all the outside folds that come from the buttons and over the edges, measuring between each fold to make sure they are all the same distance apart.

. Trim the stool with a matching braid, glueing and then sewing it in place.

Turn the stool upside-down and neaten the underside by turning in the fabric edges and tacking.

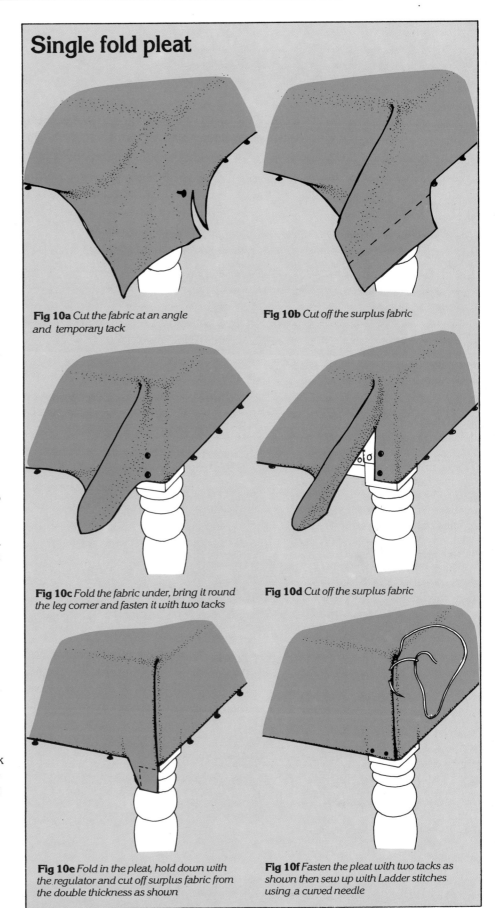

Single fold pleat

Fig 10a *Cut the fabric at an angle and temporary tack*

Fig 10b *Cut off the surplus fabric*

Fig 10c *Fold the fabric under, bring it round the leg corner and fasten it with two tacks*

Fig 10d *Cut off the surplus fabric*

Fig 10e *Fold in the pleat, hold down with the regulator and cut off surplus fabric from the double thickness as shown*

Fig 10f *Fasten the pleat with two tacks as shown then sew up with Ladder stitches using a curved needle*

Buttoned Headboard

Once you have mastered the stool top buttoning, you will want to go on to something larger, and a luxurious headboard is just the thing. You can make one to your own design and shape, or you may already possess an old headboard that requires refurbishing.

Preparation

1. Cut a piece of 13mm (1/2in) thick ply (or laminated) board to the shape desired. Pencil in the arrangement of buttons you think will be most suitable for your design. Referring to the buttoned stool top (page 56), make sure that the buttons are not too close to the edges, nor too far away.

It is well to remember that pillows will be placed against the board, so the bottom row of buttons should be placed a short distance up it.

2. When you are satisfied that the button positions give the best effect, drill 10mm (3/8in) holes in the board at the marked points. At this stage, work a tacking chamfer round the edges of the top and sides, using a wood rasp or spokeshave, because the headboard will have a stitched roll edge to it.

3. The board in the illustration (Fig 1) has the dimensions marked for a double bed size. This will have a finished covered edge of 4.5cm (1 7/8in) so the stitched edge from the tacking chamfer will be 3.5cm (1 3/8in). Carefully scribe a line round the shaped top and sides, 9cm (3 1/2in) from the edge, using the upholstery gauge. Draw another line 10cm (4in) up, parallel with the bottom edge of the board (this is as far as the upholstery will go).

Estimating the scrim hessian

4. Measure from the scribed bottom line to the centre of the curved top and add 17cm (6 3/4in) to the measurement (for forming the top edge, plus turnings). Add a further 19cm (7 1/2in) for the area below the bottom line. This gives you the total depth of scrim needed.

5. To obtain the width, measure across the headboard at its widest point, between the two scribed lines, and add 34cm (13 1/2in).

6. Cut the scrim hessian and lay it centrally on the board with 19cm (7 1/2in) lying below the bottom scribed line. With 10mm (3/8in) fine tacks, temporary tack the hessian along this line, keeping the weave straight and tacking true to the line.

7. Make sure the vertical weave is at right angles and, using the same tacks, permanently tack along the curved line at the top edge. (If you have difficulty in seeing the line through the hessian, tack the centre and the two top corners, then scribe a line on the hessian itself. Tack along this line. Set tacks about 2cm (3/4in) apart).

8. With the board lying flat and the hessian spread, cut a 14.5cm (5 3/4in) strip of thin wood to use as a measuring stick. Rest one end against the tacking line and make a series of marks against the other end. Join the marks into a continuous line.

9. Trim off the surplus hessian 2.5cm (1in) beyond the marked line. Trim the surplus hessian below the bottom line of temporary tacking, 2.5cm (1in) beyond the tacks. Do not trim right across but only as far as the ends of the rows of tacks – the remainder of the fabric is for turning the side edges.

Stuffing ties

10. In this project, the stuffing ties are fastened on pairs of 10mm (3/8in) fine tacks placed at intervals of 12.5cm (5in) across the bottom line (see Fig 2 As the ties are made, place two fingers under the loops to obtain the right degree of looseness.

Edge stuffing

11. Build up the hair firmly under the ties, forming the finished shape of the edge, and finishing at a point on the li 10cm (4in) from the bottom of the bo

12. Bring the scrim hessian over the edges, turned in to the tacking line, a tack with 10mm (3/8in) fine tacks, 2c (3/4in) apart, on the tacking chamfer. Regulate the edge well.

13. Now edge-stitch, putting in two rows of blind stitches and one row of through stitches to form an edge roll

Main stuffing

14. Fasten lines of stuffing ties acros the board between the lines of butto holes. Work the horsehair onto the board, filling up the centre area so th the surface is flat but just proud of th

---

Tools and Materials required for this project

Tools: Panel saw – coping saw, wood rasp or spokeshave, drill brace and 10mm (3/8in) bit or drill, upholstery gauge, felt tipped marker, light upholstery hammer, 10cm (4in) and 7.5cm (3in) curved needles, 25cm (10in) double pointed needle, scissors, regulator, two button fold sticks, upholstery pins and skewers, flexible steel measure. **Materials:** 13mm (1/2in) ply board, scrim hessian, horse hair, cotton wadding, polyester wadding, top fabric, buttons, backing fabric, 13mm (1/2in) improved tacks, 10mm (3/8in) fine tacks, No 3 twine, nylon button twine.

Basic skills used in this project

Stuffing ties – pages 34, 55
Fastening scrim hessian – pages 34, 55
Stuffing – pages 34, 55
Edge stitching – page 37
Buttonwork – page 58
Piping – page 40

...toned headboard made with a matching ...cover and cushions

...es.
...Cut cotton wadding into the shape ...he headboard (you may have to join ... pieces to obtain the width), and ...ead on the board. Now, cover the

wadding with a piece of polyester bonded wadding. This should be tightly stretched and taken over the board.
16. Using a regulator, pierce holes for the buttons through all the thicknesses.

Covering fabric
Joining fabric – the Van Dyke method
A double bed headboard is about

1.35m *(4ft 6in)* in width and therefore covering fabrics are not wide enough to cover a headboard in a single width. Two pieces of fabric must therefore be used and these are worked together.
17. Using tailor's chalk and a straight edge, measure and mark the button positions on the wrong side of the fabric. Pierce holes with a regulator.

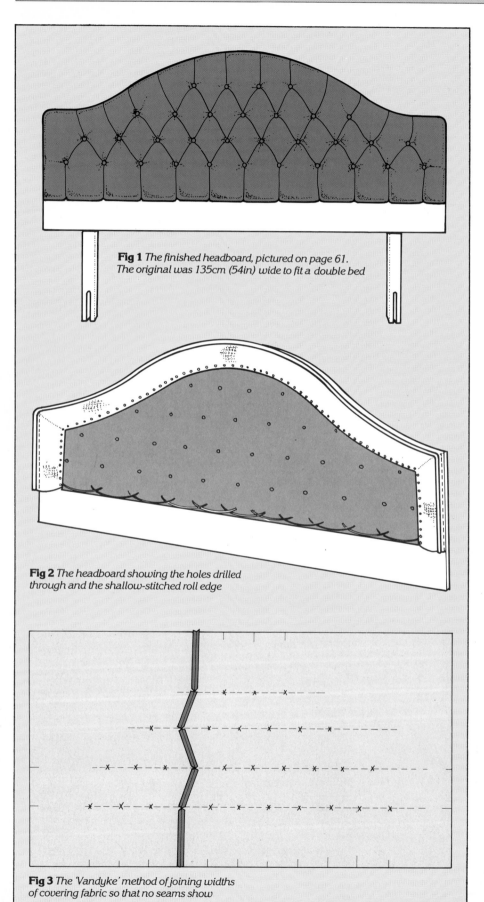

Fig 1 *The finished headboard, pictured on page 61. The original was 135cm (54in) wide to fit a double bed*

Fig 2 *The headboard showing the holes drilled through and the shallow-stitched roll edge*

Fig 3 *The 'Vandyke' method of joining widths of covering fabric so that no seams show*

18. Set out the two pieces of fabric and then cut from button mark to button mark in a zigzag, leaving a 13mm (½in) seam allowance (Fig 3). Machine-stitch the two pieces together, right sides facing, then press seams open, snipping the allowances to ease. When the buttoning is worked, the seam will be completely concealed beneath the folds.

Buttoning

At the back of the board, drive 13mm (½in) improved tacks in halfway, close to each hole. Tie the twine ends around the tacks using upholsterer's slip knots. For the time being, leave them 'unlocked'.

Begin the buttonwork by putting in the bottom row of buttons. After working the second row, fold in the diagonal pleats between the buttons, using two regulators or button fold sticks. Work the third row in the same way, fold, then finally work the top row.

19. Fold the fabric at the edges and pin the folds (refer to buttoned stool top, page 56). Temporarily tack the folds at the top and sides to the back of the board. Tack the bottom fold just below the line of edge tacks.

20. Pull all the buttons tightly, then drive home the tacks. Tighten, then permanently tack down all the outside fold pleats. Tack the fabric between the folds but do not tension it.

21. Cover the 10cm (4in) of bare board at the bottom of the board with an overlay of cotton wadding. Cut a strip of covering fabric to fit it, adding an allowance for turning onto the back of the board. Stretch the fabric and turn the edges. Ladder-stitch the seam at the top edge of the strip where it joins the padded area.

Finishing

22. Make up a length of piping, long enough to go round the sides and the top, and pin this in place, slightly overlapping the edge. Cut a piece of cotton wadding to fit the back of the headboard. Lay this in place.

23. Cut a piece of calico or lining for the back, plus a turning allowance. Turn in the edges and pin. Sew the piping and the back fabric in place with ladder stitches.

24. Screw the support stands to the back of the headboard, ready to be fixed to the bed.

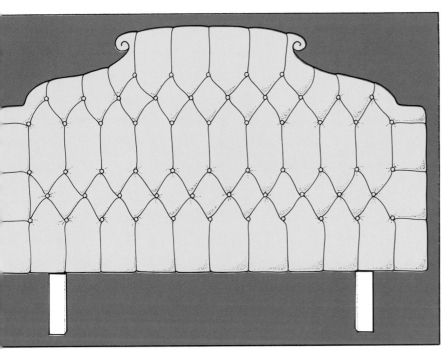

Fig 4 *A more elaborate buttoning arrangement on a decoratively-shaped headboard*

Once you have mastered the fascinating craft of upholstery, you will be able to create beautiful furnishings schemes for your home. This elegant padded bedhead has a pleated border, edged with piping. The fabric is matched to a fitted bed cover, an Austrian window blind and frilled and quilted cushions.

Trinket box

Relining a box interior is another upholstery job you will want to try. Start with a small wooden trinket box, like the one illustrated.

Materials required

Thin, stiff cardboard
Thin polyester wadding
Silk or cotton fabric
Thixotropic impact adhesive
Small beads, sewing thread (optional)

Preparation

Remove the old lining, glue, etc and clean the box thoroughly. Measure the inside panels of the box, four sides, bottom and inside lid. Draw these shapes to size on the thin cardboard. Draw a second line 3mm (⅛in) inside the first. Cut out the card shapes on the inside line.

Place the cards on the wadding and cut 9mm (⅜in) larger all round. Place the cards on the fabric and cut out 18mm (¾in) larger all round.

Making the lining

Spread the fabric wrong side up and place the wadding on top, centring it. Centre the card on top. Spread a thin line of glue along the card edges (see Fig 1). Turn the fabric and wadding on the card, pressing it onto the glue and mitring the corners (see Fig 1). Cover each piece of card in the same way. Leave to dry under weights.

Assembly

The padded cards are glued to the inside of the box. Spread a line of glue round the padded cards on the wrong sides (see Fig 2) and press each in place inside the box. Leave to dry.

The inside of the lid can be decorated with beads if you like. Use a slightly thicker card and mark the positions of the beads on the wrong side before covering the card. Pierce holes on the hole positions. After the padding has been completed, thread a needle with strong thread. Pass the needle through a hole from the wrong side, through the padding and fabric. Slip a bead onto the needle and slide it down onto the thread. Pass the needle back through the padding and through the hole in the cardboard (see Fig 3). Cut the thread end and tie the ends in a double knot. Spread a little glue on the knots.

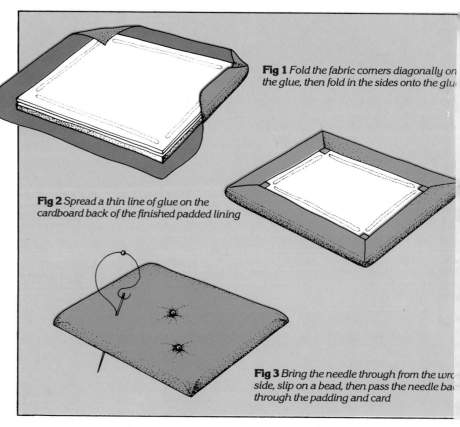

Fig 1 *Fold the fabric corners diagonally on the glue, then fold in the sides onto the glue*

Fig 2 *Spread a thin line of glue on the cardboard back of the finished padded lining*

Fig 3 *Bring the needle through from the wrong side, slip on a bead, then pass the needle back through the padding and card*